Reprint Series No. 2

CROCHET DESIGNS

Classic Fashions from 1920s & 1930s

REPRINTED FROM ORIGINAL SOURCES

Compiled by

Margaret Deshmane

for the

Knitting and Crochet Guild

KNITTING AND CROCHET GUILD

London

1990

ACKNOWLEDGEMENTS

The Knitting and Crochet Guild wishes to express its deep appreciation to Lady Scott, Patron of the Guild, for her encouragement and generous support, without which the work could not have been completed. Many other members of the Guild have contributed to the project through their interest in crochet work and its history, and we can name only a few who have made special contributions of their time, experience and skills: Gertrude Kuehl, Sue Leighton-White, Jo Olley, Sheila Ryle, Anita Schuetz, Barbara Tennant, Mavis Walker and all those who have kindly agreed to crochet designs for exhibition.

First published in Great Britain in 1990
by the Knitting and Crochet Guild
47 Yarmouth Rd., Ormesby St. Margaret
Great Yarmouth, Norfolk NR29 3QE
Charity registration No. 802465

The designs contained in this book have been reprinted in facsimile from the original sources quoted in the Table of Contents. Part of the intrinsic interest of these historic designs is their original presentation and in the interests of authenticity these designs have been reproduced directly from the originals without comment or amendment. No responsibility, therefore, can be accepted for any errors existing in the original designs. It should also be noted that any defects in the standard of reproduction reflect those of the original sources.

British Library Cataloguing in Publication Data
Crochet designs: classic fashions from 1920's & 1930s.
I Crocheting
I. Deshmane, Margaret II. Knitting and Crochet Guild 746. 434

ISBN 0-951349I-2-0

Printed in Great Britain by Crowes Printers, 11 Concorde Road,
Norwich NR6 6BJ.

CONTENTS

FOREWORD

As the pace and pressures of modern life increase, there is greater risk of overlooking the value of art and crafts in our daily lives. The Knitting and Crochet Guild has begun the last decade of the 20th century with new responsibilities as a registered charity and renewed dedication to promoting excellence and keeping alive for future generations the skills of crochet and machine and hand knitting.

As with many crafts, crochet has known periods or cycles of high and low popularity. Following the Edwardian period when crochet lace was much in vogue, interest in the craft declined for a decade or more, but soon revived with renewed interest in fabric crochet.

These reprinted designs illustrate how easily crochet can respond to current fashion trends once the basic techniques are understood. Many of the designs in this period have such classic styling they will appeal immediately to the modern fashion-conscious woman, and those which illustrate interesting crochet techniques can easily be adapted to modern needs.

I hope this booklet will help re-introduce crochet to women of all ages and will restore the craft to a level of prominence in the fashion world of the 1990s.

Anne Scott

Lady Scott

INTRODUCTION

It has often been remarked that interest in crochet waxes and wanes. The first half of the 1920s was a time of great interest in crocheted garments: patterns for jumpers, jackets, blouses and dresses appeared in the magazines and booklets, enabling women to adopt the new fashion for a loose, straight look that followed the First World War. But in the second half of the 1920s, when Chanel and Schiaparelli introduced knitwear to high fashion and high society, crochet seems to have been overshadowed by the exciting developments in knitting. It was not until the early 1930s when Paris took up crochet as well that interest revived. By then the styles were quite different – close fitting and short-waisted.

In this selection of crochet patterns from the period between the Wars the focus is on women's garments, most of which are suitable for making as they stand. A few items have been included mainly for historical interest, to serve as inspiration and to show what can be done with crochet. But virtually everything in the book can be tackled by those with some experience, provided they are willing to spend a little more time on preparation than would normally be necessary for a contemporary pattern.

How to use the book

The designs in this book demonstrate vividly what different meanings attach to those words "to fit bust 36 inches" at different times. In the early 1920s, as in the 1980s, the actual size of such a garment could be as much as 46 inches, as you will see from the quoted advice of the period on page 8, and patterns such as those on pages 10/11 and 16 – 18. But in the 1930s the fit was very much closer; two inches ease at the most and often none at all, or even tight – 30 inches to fit 34 inches – no doubt essential when pure wool was used in the swimsuit on page 29. Moreover, diagrams which enabled the worker to see at a glance the shape and size and thus where adjustments might be required are no longer provided in the instructions. Instead, a careful reading of the pattern and calculations from the given tension (if any) are required to decide what the actual measurements are, a situation which all too often is still the same today.

Having chosen a pattern in a style you like, which appears to be suitable in size, or can be easily adjusted, the next step is to find a yarn of an appropriate type and thickness to give a good result. The size of hook specified in the pattern, together with the tension shown, will give an idea of where to start, as will the table provided. Remember that, even where the yarn used in the original may seem to be available today (e.g. 4-ply wool), the 1930s yarn may not be comparable to the contemporary yarn. Over the years the thickness has changed, so look around and experiment. A good source of finer yarns are those made for machine knitters. Ask a machine knitting friend to let you have some leftovers to play around with – you may be pleasantly surprised at the result. And look in craft suppliers for things such as artificial raffia, macrame twine, or in the stationers for brightly coloured man-made "string".

When experimenting it is absolutely essential to make a piece of fabric large enough to allow your tension to settle down in order to give a true result. Make it in the stitch to be used for the item, as the same yarn worked in different stitches can give a dramatically different effect. Depending on the yarn, the swatch may also need washing and/or blocking if you are to see what will really happen when the garment is finished.

Certain other points should be borne in mind when considering the possible suitability of a yarn for a specific pattern. If the original depends on a crisp, firm finish for its effect, it will look totally different if you use a soft or a fluffy yarn. (The result may, of course, be satisfactory – but it will not be the same). And take particular care, especially if the garment is already close fitting, if you substitute an inelastic yarn for a very elastic one, such as cotton for pure wool.

But don't be afraid to change and adapt the patterns to what you want. This book has been published in response to the request of many crocheters who want to make clothes to wear today, not for display in a museum. It may take a little more time and effort to get started, but I am sure you will be pleased with the result, which will be individual and interesting. So – good luck!

Margaret Deshmane

January 1990

NOTES

Stitches
The basic stitches are illustrated on page 32. American readers should remember that what in the UK is called 'double crochet' is for them 'single crochet' and similarly 'treble crochet' is for them 'double crochet'. The 'long treble' (p. 21) is a 'double treble' (or 'treble' in the U.S.).

Hooks
Prior to metrication in 1969, different manufacturers in the UK used different sizing systems for their hooks. Unfortunately, most of the books that give comparative tables of the old and new sizes neither explain this, nor specify which manufacturer's sizing is given. Such comparison tables can be more confusing than helpful. The table on the inside front cover gives the size range used in the patterns in this book. On p. 29 'tricot' is an older term for 'tunisian'.

THIS quickly made jumper is worked throughout in double crochet. The lower portion, the cuffs, and collar are worked in ribbed double crochet, taking up the back thread of each stitch always, and the body portion and the sleeves are worked in plain double crochet, taking up both threads of every stitch.

The garment measures about 34 inches round the ribbed edge without stretching, 15 inches long at underarm seam, entire length 24 inches, and sleeve seam 19 inches. If preferred the collar could be dispensed with, and a small edging worked all round the opening at neck and down front.

MATERIALS.

One and a quarter pounds of Messrs. Baldwin & Walker's 4-ply Ladyship Primrose Fleecy Wool, and a bone crochet hook size 5.

THE FRONT.

Commence the ribbed portion with 34 chain, miss one chain, 1 d.c. into every stitch, 1 ch., turn, * 1 d.c. into the back thread of every stitch, 1 ch., turn, and repeat from *, making the same number of stitches in each row, and keeping the edges straight and level until there are sixty-two rows made, which will show thirty-one ribs of double crochet. Now work along the ends of these rows of ribbing for the body portion of the garment. Work 1 d.c. into the end of every rib and 1 d.c. into the space between the ribs until there are thirty-one stitches made, and this is the centre of the front of the jumper where the opening commences, 1 ch., turn, * 1 d.c. into every stitch to the end, taking up two threads of each stitch always. Repeat from * until there are twenty-eight rows worked on to the ribbing, and the wool is at the side of the garment ready to commence the sleeve.

THE LEFT SLEEVE.

Work 63 chain for the sleeve and cuff, which are worked at the same time. This chain should measure about 21 inches, and not be tightly worked.

1st row—Miss one chain, 1 d.c. into every stitch to end of chain, and now work on across the body portion to end, making ninety-three stitches all along the row, 1 ch., turn.

2nd row—1 d.c. into each of the first seventy-five stitches, now for the cuff work 1 d.c. into the back thread of each of the last eighteen stitches to make the ribbing, 1 ch., turn.

3rd row—Rib the first eighteen stitches 1 d.c. into every stitch to end, 1 ch., turn.

4th row—1 d.c. into every stitch until the ribbing is reached, then do not work on the cuff, but leave it this time, and make 1 ch., turn.

5th row—Miss one double crochet, 1 d.c. into every stitch to end, 1 ch., turn.

6th row—1 d.c. into every stitch, 1 d.c. into the one chain at end, then pass along on to the cuff and work 1 d.c. into the back thread of the eighteen stitches, 1 ch., turn.

7th row—Rib the first eighteen stitches for cuff, 1 d.c. into each of the remaining seventy-five stitches.

Now repeat the last four rows five times more, and the piece should measure about 7 inches. Work the cuff portion in this manner to end of directions for sleeve, always working a short row between the long rows. Do not break off the wool, but leave it hanging here, and work the right side of the garment.

Commence again at the opposite end of the ribbing, and work 1 d.c. into the end of each row until there are thirty-one double crochet, and the centre opening is reached. Continue backwards and forwards for

The ribbing at lower edge of front of Jumper is worked first and done shortways as here shown.

twenty-eight rows, then work 63 ch. for sleeve, and work in same manner as on first half, and fasten off.

Now take up the wool that was left hanging on first half, and make 9 ch., pass over to second portion and work 1 d.c. through two threads of every stitch all down the right sleeve (the nine chain are for the back of the neck), always remembering to keep the cuffs the same as on first portion of sleeve.

Next row—1 d.c. into every stitch from side to side, working into the nine chain across back.

Now work backwards and forwards along the whole length of the sleeves, and back, and decreasing one stitch (to decrease insert hook into next stitch, draw wool through, insert hook into next stitch, draw wool through, wool over, and draw through all loops on the hook with one stitch, thus merging two stitches into one) in the middle of every alternate row, but do not decrease in the same place every time, anywhere along the back between the sleeves, until there are eighteen rows to be seen at the back counting down from the nine chain that span across the neck, and nine stitches less than in the first.

The double crochet stitch for body part of Jumper is the same both sides of the work, as two threads of each stitch are always taken up.

Next row—Work the sleeve and across back until within twenty stitches from the top of the cuff (thirty-eight stitches from extreme end of row), leave these twenty stitches unworked, and make 1 ch., turn.

Next row—Miss one double crochet, 1 d.c. into each stitch up sleeve and across back, down next sleeve until within twenty stitches of top of cuff here stop, and work 1 ch., turn.

Next row—1 d.c. into every stitch right across until within twelve stitches of end of short row last made, leave these stitches, and work 1 ch., turn.

Next row—Miss one stitch, 1 d.c. into every stitch until within twelve stitches of end of short row last made on this sleeve, leave these stitches, and work 1 ch., turn.

Next row—1 d.c. into every stitch to end of row, working into the one chain at the end of the short rows and continuing to end, always remembering to keep the cuff correct.

Now work three more rows across the entire garment from cuff to cuff, when there must be 186 stitches in the row. Fasten off.

THE BACK.

Hold the garment with the last row of double crochet made with the wrong side of it uppermost, miss 62 stitches along sleeve, then work 1 d.c. into each of the next sixty-two stitches, 1 ch., turn, leaving the last sixty-two stitches unused.

Now work rows of double crochet (taking up two threads always) backwards and forwards on these sixty-two stitches, until the back is the same length as the front measuring by putting the two sides of the sleeve together. Do not break off, but work lower portion of back.

FOR THE RIBBING AT BACK.

Make 34 chain, miss one chain, 1 d.c. into every stitch to end, 1 ch., turn, 1 d.c. into back thread of every stitch, 1 d.c. into the first stitch along the edge of the last row of back, 1 d.c. into next stitch along row, turn, * miss the last two double crochet made, 1 d.c. into the back thread of every stitch of previous row, 1 ch., turn, 1 d.c. into the back thread of every stitch, 1 d.c. into the next stitch on last row of back, 1 d.c. into next stitch along row, turn, and repeat from * to end. Fasten off.

THE COLLAR.

Commence with 13 chain.

1st row—Miss one chain, 1 d.c. into every stitch, 1 ch., turn.

2nd row—1 d.c. into the back thread of every stitch, 1 ch., turn, and repeat the 2nd row until there are twenty rows worked, showing ten ribs.

21st row—* 1 d.c. into each of the first six stitches, slip-stitch into next stitch (to slip-stitch insert hook into next stitch and draw wool through stitch, and loop on hook at same time), turn.

22nd row—Miss the slip-stitch, 1 d.c. into the back thread of each of the next six stitches, 1 ch., turn.

23rd row—1 d.c. into back thread of first six stitches, 1 d.c. into same place as slip-stitch, 1 d.c. into back thread of remaining stitches.

Work three rows right across, taking up the back thread always, then repeat from * in 21st row six times. Work twenty rows as at commencement, and fasten off.

For the cord take the wool double and work a chain measuring about 40 inches.

TO MAKE UP THE JUMPER.

Sew up seams under arm and down sleeve, drawing the edges together, and matching up the ribbing evenly at waist and cuffs.

Place the centre of collar to centre of back of neck, and sew on right side, so that when the collar is turned back the stitches are invisible. Sew the front opening together above ribbing for 2 or 3 inches. Thread the cord up front, and sew tassels to each end of it. Attach a small tassel to each end of collar, or tack corners down to avoid curling.

THE professional look—isn't that what all the industrious amateurs who are knitting or crocheting jumpers desire for their finished work? What a pity so few obtain it! There's no earthly reason why they shouldn't if they'll only follow the hints which I am able to give them from my own experience as a West End designer.

The first essential is either a paper pattern or a correct set of measurements to work from. Of course, if you are copying any of the designs in this book, you can draw out a full-size pattern according to the measurements on the diagram.

When making a pattern for a special size, add not less than 6 ins. to the person's actual bust measure, or even 8 ins. or 10 ins., if she desires a very loose fit. Remember that a jumper should always hang gracefully from the shoulders, and should not be tight round the bust, or the effect is very ugly. For exceptional figures, where the front width is much in excess of the back, the front part of the jumper may be wider than the back, being gradually enlarged at the sides from the bottom upwards, or the front may be made 1½ ins. longer than the back and the extra length eased in at the seams.

Note that the sleeve should always be exactly in the centre of the side of the jumper when it is flat on the table.

Very effective jumpers may be made of crochet medallions, either square, round, or oval. These may be made at odd moments and then arranged on the paper pattern, afterwards being sewn plainly together or joined with fancy stitches.

No. 6816.—The "LINSLADE" CROCHET COAT.

Abbreviations: Ch., chain; sl.st., slip stitch; d.c., double crochet; tr., treble.

FOURTEEN large balls of Ardern's "Star Sylko," No. 3, Shade 811, Mid. Violet, were used for this Coat, a crochet hook size 0, and three button moulds.

The body of the garment is worked in double crochet, surrounded by rows of chain and treble, then the side seams laced up and the sleeves set in. Bust measurement thirty-seven inches.

Begin at the back panel with 57 ch..

1st row. 1 d.c. in each stitch, missing the first, making 56 d.c..

2nd row. 1 d.c. in each stitch, putting the hook through both loops and working 1 or 2 ch. for first always.

Repeat the 2nd row till the panel measures twelve and a half inches long; the d.c. are worked tightly, and the work should be ten and a quarter inches across. The approximate number of stitches is given, but they should be altered if necessary to suit the requirements of the worker.

Continue working in same stitch, but decrease a stitch at the beginning (by slip stitching back 1 stitch) and at the end (by not working into end one); continue in this way till about four and a half inches are done. The panel should measure seventeen inches long.

Work only 13 d.c. in next 2 rows for right-hand shoulder; 12 d.c. in next 2 rows; 11 d.c. in next 8; and 10 in next 14.

(continued p. 9)

Now begin to increase, work 11 d.c. in next 6 rows (putting 2 in first stitch of first row of 6); 13 d.c. in next 6 rows (putting 2 in first stitch of first and second rows of 6); 15 d.c. in next 4 rows (increasing as before, this is understood); 17 d.c. in next 6 rows; 19 in next 6; 21 in next 6; 23 in next 6; 25 in next 6; 27 in next 6; 29 in next 6; 31 in next 4; 33 in next, and 34 for about eight more inches; cut and fasten off the "Sylko."

Miss 30 d.c. on back panel, join to next stitch, and work the other shoulder and front to correspond; from shoulder to bottom of front panel should measure twenty and three-quarter inches. The rows round the body of coat are now worked, they should be done rather loosely, but must lie flat.

1st row. Join "Sylko" to point of back panel. 1 d.c., 3 ch. and 1 d.c. in same place, * 2 ch., miss 2 ch. below, 1 d.c. in next, repeat from * across back, at the next point work 1 d.c., 3 ch., and 1 d.c., then continue up the side with 2 ch., miss 2 d.c. rows, 1 d.c. in next. Work all round in this way, and join the row with a slip stitch.

2nd row. 3 tr. (3 ch. for first), 1 ch., and 3 tr. in 3 ch. at point, and 3 tr. under each loop of 2 ch., repeat all round, and join.

3rd row. 1 d.c., 3 ch. and 1 d.c. under 1 ch. at a point, 2 ch., 1 d.c. between next 2 groups of 3 tr., repeat and join.

4th row. 3 tr., 1 ch., and 3 tr. at a point, then 3 tr. under each loop of 2 ch..

Repeat the 3rd and 4th rows 3 times, then the 3rd again, but making 3 buttonholes of 4 ch., and missing 2 groups below, about five inches apart, and finish by working d.c. closely into each loop, fasten off.

No. 6816.—THE "LINSLADE" CROCHET COAT.

SLEEVE.

This is worked in two pieces, begin with 106 ch. for the Insertion, which runs from shoulder to edge of sleeve.

1st row. 2 ch., miss 2 stitches, 1 d.c. in next, repeat making 35 loops.

2nd row. 3 tr. (3 ch. for first) in each loop.

3rd row. 2 ch. and 1 d.c. between each tr. group.

Repeat the 2nd and 3rd rows six times.

16th row. 2 d.c. in 2 ch. loop, 1 d.c. in d.c., making 105 d.c..

17th to 21st row. 1 d.c. in each stitch.

22nd row. 1 d.c. in each stitch except the 2 last (103 d.c.), this is the shoulder end.

23rd row. 1 d.c. in each stitch.

Repeat the last 2 rows six times.

36th row. 1 d.c. in each stitch except the last.

37th row. 1 d.c. in each stitch except the last 20, this is the cuff end.

38th row. 1 d.c. in each stitch.

39th row. 1 d.c. in each stitch except the last 10.

40th row. 1 d.c. in each stitch.

Repeat the 39th and 40th rows five times.

Break off thread, join again to the other side of Insertion at the shoulder end and work the other part of sleeve.

1st row. Like the 16th row of first part.

2nd to 6th row. Like the 17th to 21st row.

7th row. Sl.st. back along 2 stitches, and finish with d.c..

8th row. Like the 23rd.

Repeat the last 2 rows six times.

21st row. Sl.st. back along 1 stitch and finish with d.c..

22nd row. Sl.st. back along 20 stitches and finish with d.c..

23rd row. Like the 38th row.

24th row. Sl.st. back along 10 stitches and finish with d.c..

25th row. Like the 40th.

Repeat the 24th and 25th rows five times and fasten off.

LACING.

Make a chain about one and three-quarter yards long, turn, work sl.st. along it, fasten off; double this cord and lace the front and back of coat together; leaving room for the sleeve, finish each end with a "bob."

"BOB."

Begin with 4 ch., join into ring with a sl.st., then work d.c. round and round, increasing by working 2 stitches into 1, till it measures three-quarters of an inch in diameter, fill with cotton wool, and decrease by missing a stitch occasionally till it is closed up, then sew to end of cord. Whip up the sleeves and sew into armhole, putting the seam one and a half inches from side join, towards the front, and catching back and front, also cord, together.

BUTTON.

Begin with 3 ch., join, and work d.c. round and round, increasing till large enough, slip the button mould in and decrease like the "bob." Finally sew on the buttons opposite the buttonholes.

CHARMING AND UP-TO-THE-MINUTE

is this jumper of Maltese crochet in fine silk, giving the effect of exquisite lace

Materials.—*Thirty ½ oz. balls of Rickards' "Sylvan" fine knitting silk, or eight 2-oz. reels of Cullen's "Elfin" artificial silk, 2 yds. of black moiré ribbon ½-in. wide, and a steel crochet hook No. 3.*
Measurements.—*Length from top of shoulder, 25 ins.; width round the bust, 45 ins.; width round the basque, 42 ins.; length of sleeve from the neck, 8 ins.*
Tension.—*5 spaces to an inch, measured across the work.*
Abbreviations.—*Ch. = chain; d.c. = double crochet; sp. = space; tr. = treble; d.tr. = double treble.*

THE original fits a figure with from 32 to 36-inch bust measurement.

THE jumper is made in 18 strips—9 for the back and 9 for the front, and joined on the shoulders. Ten of these strips are in Maltese crochet, and 8 are in spaces edged with treble.

THE MALTESE STRIPS.

Make a chain of about 41.

1st row—Silk twice over hook and put hook into 5th ch. along, draw the silk through, making 4 loops on hook. Silk over and draw through 2 loops, silk over and draw through 2 more loops, leaving 2 loops on hook; silk over twice and put hook into same stitch as before and draw through a loop, making 5 loops on hook. Now put silk over and draw through 2 loops, silk over and draw through the last 3 loops. This makes 1 leaf. 5 ch. and repeat from the beginning, starting with silk twice over hook, and putting the hook into the first of the 5 ch. just made. When the second leaf is completed, catch it with a d.c. into the 7th ch. along. * Make two more leaves and catch into the 7th ch. along. Repeat from * 3 times, making 5 sets of leaves altogether. Turn with 3 leaves.

2nd row—Catch with a d.c. into the middle of the first two leaves, * make 2 leaves, catch into the middle of the next 2 leaves. Repeat from * 3 times to the end. Turn with 3 leaves. Repeat this last row for a length of 17 ins., and turn with 1 leaf, then make * 7 ch., 1 d.c. between 2 leaves. Repeat from * to the end of the row, and continue the same along the side edge. Join on silk at the other side edge and repeat.

Make 9 more strips in the same way.

THE SPACES AND TREBLE STRIPS.

Make a ch. of about 259.

1st row—1 tr. into the 3rd ch. from hook, then 1 tr. into each ch. to the end, making 256 altogether. (This row should measure 17 ins.) Turn with 5 ch.

2nd row—Miss 2 tr., 1 tr. into next, * 2 ch., miss 2 tr., 1 tr. into next. Repeat from * making 85 sp. altogether.

3rd to 6th rows—As 2nd.

7th row—256 tr.

Make 7 more strips in the same way.

Press all the strips on the wrong side with a hot iron over a damp cloth, and see that they are all the same length. Take 1 Maltese strip for the centre front and stitch a narrow strip on each side of it. Now stitch a Maltese strip on each side of these, another narrow strip on each side, then a Maltese strip for the outside edges. Use the other 9 strips in the same way for the back.

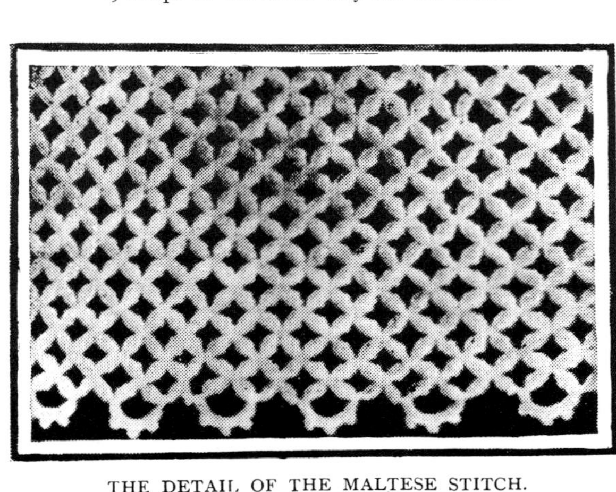

THE DETAIL OF THE MALTESE STITCH.

QUITE SIMPLE TO COPY

Along the top edge of the front work thus :—

1st row—7 tr. into the 7 ch. between the leaves, 1 tr. into the d.c. Repeat from * to the end of the Maltese strip, then 22 tr. over the narrow strip. Repeat from * to the end.

2nd and 3rd rows—All spaces.

4th row—Work spaces along for $4\frac{3}{4}$ ins. only for the shoulder. Turn.

5th row—Work tr. to the end and break off. Go back to the other end of the front and work spaces along for $4\frac{3}{4}$ ins., turn and work tr. to the end. Break off. Along the top of the back work a row of tr. right across as for the front, then 3 rows of spaces right across and break off. Press, then join the shoulders and side seams, leaving armholes 12 ins. all round (or larger if preferred).

THE SLEEVES.

Work 1 round of tr., 5 rounds of spaces, and 1 round of tr.

THE MALTESE SLEEVE EDGING.

This is made separately and then stitched on afterwards. Make 2 rows of 6 leaves in each row (this means 3 sets of 2 leaves).

3rd row—6 leaves, then 1 leaf, 10 ch. Catch with a d.c. into the middle of the two end leaves of the previous rows. Turn.

** **4th row**—Work 4 d.c., 4 ch., 4 d.c., 4 ch., 4 d.c., 4 ch., 4 d.c., into the loop of 10 ch., * 2 leaves, catch into the middle of next 2 leaves. Repeat from * twice to the end. Turn with 3 leaves.

5th and 6th rows—3 sets of 2 leaves in each row.

7th row—Same as 3rd row.

Repeat from ** for length required, then work a row of ch. along the bottom edge to be sewn to the sleeve.

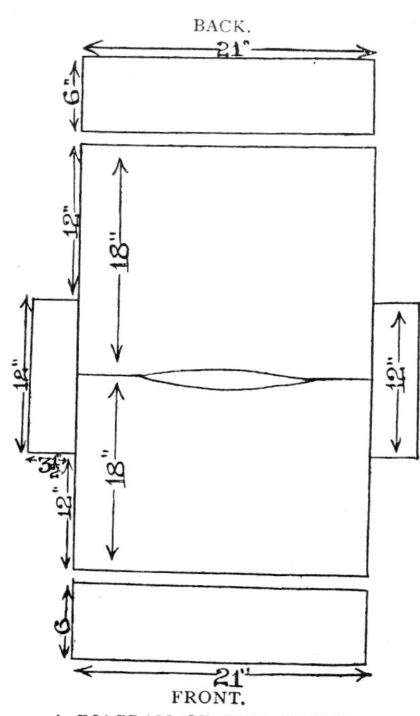

A DIAGRAM OF THE JUMPER.

THE COLLAR.

Make a strip of about 36 ins. as for the sleeve edging, but work 14 leaves in width. Along the edge to be sewn to the neck work 1 d.c. in the middle of every 2 leaves with 2 ch. between. This will gather up the collar. Now work a row of d.c. and break off. Work a row of d.c. all round the neck edge, missing a stitch at intervals to shape. Press the collar and stitch on.

THE WAIST STRIP.

Work 1 round of tr. to the lower edge of the jumper, 1 round of spaces, then a round of large spaces thus :—

1 d.tr. (twice over hook) into the 1st tr., * 5 ch., miss 2 sp., 1 d.tr. into next tr. Repeat from *. One more round of small spaces, 1 round of tr., and press.

THE BASQUE.

Make a strip of Maltese edging to reach all round the waist, the depth being just the same as for the collar. Work a row of ch. along the top to stitch to the waist strip.

THE GIRDLE.

Cut about 24 strands of silk each about 2 yds. in length, and tie a knot at one end. Hold the knot in the left hand and divide the strands in half. * With the right thumb and finger twist 12 strands tightly away from you and hold down with the left hand. Twist the other 12 strands tightly in the same way, and hold down over the first twisted strands. Repeat from * to the end, then tie another knot. Thread through the large spaces at the waist. Finish off the ends with tassels.

Wear a black moiré ribbon bow with long ends at the neck.

Abbreviations : ch., chain; d.c., double crochet.

Materials : Two 80-yard skeins W.B. Raffia-sil Twist.
A small quantity of 3 ply wool.
A Stratnoid crochet hook, No. 14.
A buckle.

Measurements : 37 inches long; $1\frac{3}{4}$ inches wide.

THE BELT.

USING **raffia,** commence with 15 chain. **1st row**—Miss 1 ch., 14 d.c., 1 ch., turn. Work rows of 14 d.c. until strip measures 36 inches. **Next row**—Miss 1 d.c., 11 d.c., miss 1 d.c., 1 d.c., 1 ch., turn. **Next 4 rows**—Miss 1 d.c., 1 d.c. on every d.c. until 2 remain, miss 1 d.c., 1 d.c., 1 ch., turn. **Next row**—4 d.c., 1 ch., turn.

Next row—4 d.c. Fasten off. With wool, work a row of double crochet all round belt.

The Slot.—Using raffia, commence with 4 ch., then miss 1 ch., 3 d.c., 1 ch., turn. Work rows of 3 d.c. until strip measures 4 inches. Fasten off and sew ends together. Sew on buckle and pass belt through slot.

A CROCHET POCHETTE IN ARTIFICIAL SILK RAFFIA.

Abbreviations : ch., chain; d.c., double crochet.

Materials : One 1-ounce hank Vicars' Salome Artificial silk raffia. (Black.)
Vicars' Salome Raffia Artificial Silk Embroidery, in small skeins, 6 pink, 3 red, 4 dark green, 1 pale green.
A Stratnoid crochet hook, No. 16.
$\frac{3}{4}$ yard Jap silk, $\frac{1}{2}$ yard black canvas.
1 patent fastener.
Wadding for padding.

Measurements : 12 inches by 6 inches.

Description : *This very useful pochette is worked throughout in double crochet, with a spray of roses on front.*

USING black raffia, commence with 127 chain. **1st row**—Miss 1 ch., 126 d.c., 1 ch., turn.

Next 17 rows—126 d.c., 1 ch., turn. Now work according to chart from 19th row, stranding raffia not in use at back of work.

Next 132 rows—126 d.c., 1 ch., turn. Fasten off.

The strap.—Using black raffia, commence with 10 chain. **1st row**—Miss 1 ch., 9 d.c., 1 ch., turn. Work rows of 9 d.c. for 2 inches and fasten off.

TO MAKE UP.

Press well on wrong side under a damp cloth with a hot iron. Sew to canvas (putting a layer of wadding covered with silk between the canvas and crochet), and line with silk. Turn up bottom of pochette for 6 inches, and sew up sides. Sew strap to back of pochette at lower edge, and fasten to front with a patent fastener.

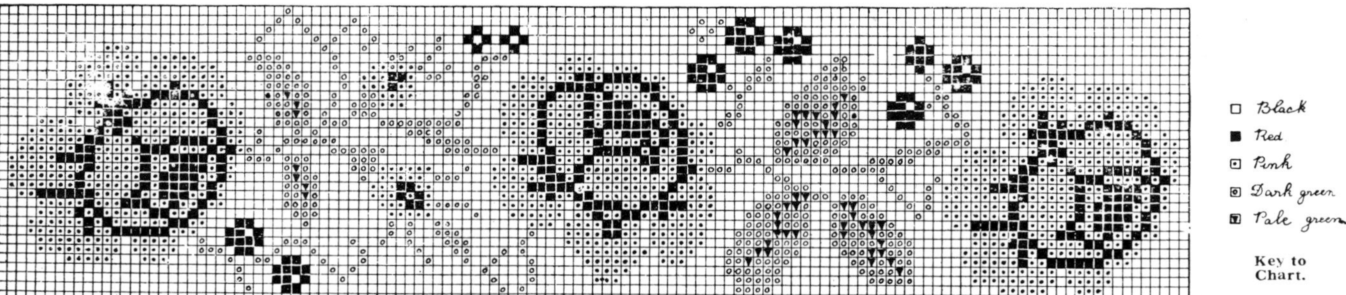

Bags always make most acceptable gifts. There are directions for making Knitted, Crochet, Bead, Embroidered and Ribbon Bags and Pochettes in Weldon's Sixpenny Series, No. 125, by post 7d.

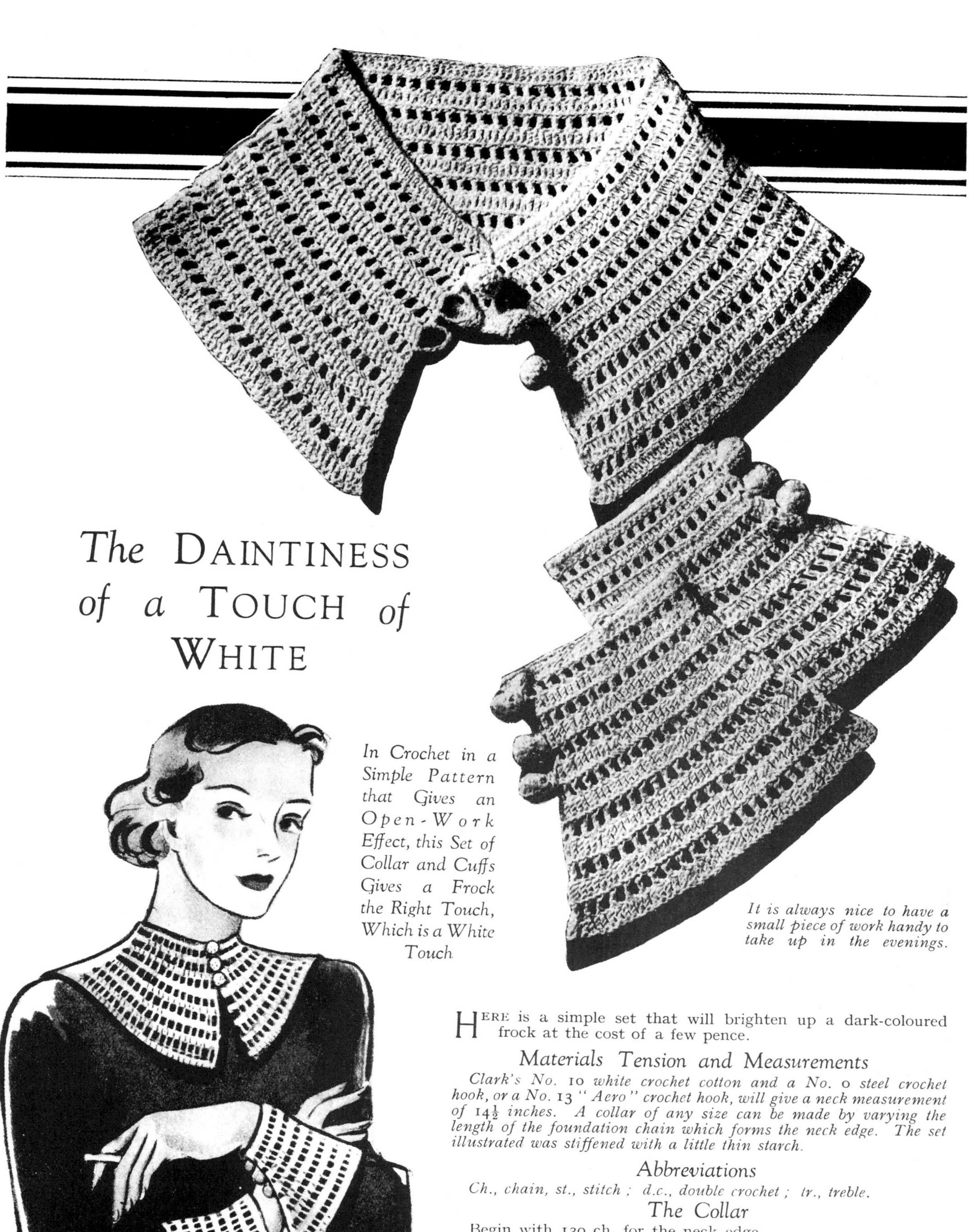

The DAINTINESS of a TOUCH of WHITE

In Crochet in a Simple Pattern that Gives an Open-Work Effect, this Set of Collar and Cuffs Gives a Frock the Right Touch, Which is a White Touch

It is always nice to have a small piece of work handy to take up in the evenings.

HERE is a simple set that will brighten up a dark-coloured frock at the cost of a few pence.

Materials Tension and Measurements

Clark's No. 10 white crochet cotton and a No. 0 steel crochet hook, or a No. 13 " Aero " crochet hook, will give a neck measurement of 14½ inches. A collar of any size can be made by varying the length of the foundation chain which forms the neck edge. The set illustrated was stiffened with a little thin starch.

Abbreviations

Ch., chain, st., stitch ; d.c., double crochet ; tr., treble.

The Collar

Begin with 130 ch. for the neck edge.

1st row : 1 tr. in the 4th ch. from the hook, then 1 tr. in each remaining ch., making 128 trs. along the row, counting the 3 ch. at the beginning as 1 tr., 4 ch., turn.

2nd row : The 4 ch. which turned the previous row now counts as 1 tr. and 1 ch., so miss the first 2 tr., 1 tr. on the next tr., taking up both loops at the top of the st. throughout the work, * 1 ch., miss 1 tr., 1 tr. on the next tr. and repeat from * to the end of the row, and work the last tr. into the top of the 3 ch. at this end of the row, 3 ch., turn.

3rd row : Miss the first tr., then 1 tr. in each st. (ch. and tr.) to end of row, 4 ch., turn.

Repeat the 2nd and 3rd row 6 times more, but to shape the collar increase on the tr. rows as follows :

On the *5th row :* (3rd tr. row) increase by working 2 trs. in every 12th st.

7th row : Increase as on the 5th row.

9th row : Increase in every 13th stitch.

11th row : Increase in every 17th stitch.

13th row : As 11th row.

15th row : Increase in every 18th st. and fasten off.

Make 3 crochet loops thus : 1 d.c. into the top of the tr. on the second row from the neck edge on the right side of the collar, 8 ch., 1 d.c. at the base of the tr. on the next row below. Make 2 loops more, spanning the 4th and 5th row and the 6th and 7th row below.

THE CROCHET BUTTONS.—Make a loop by winding the cotton twice round the little finger, leaving the cut end free ; make 4 d.c. into this loop, and draw up the end of the cotton closely, 2 d.c. into every st. on the previous round, making 8 d.c. Work 3 rounds more, increasing twice only on the round. Stuff this little cup with cotton wool, then decrease by working into every alternate st. only until the cup is closed. Fasten off securely.

Make two buttons more and sew on the left side of the collar opposite the loops.

The Cuffs

Begin with 64 ch. for the wrist edge, and work exactly as described for the collar, getting 62 trs. on the first row. Work the open row, then repeat these two rows once more with exactly the same number of stitches.

5th row (tr. row) : Increase in the first st., then increase in every 10th st. along the row and again in the last st.

Work the open row as usual.

7th row : As 5th row.

9th row : Increase in every 12th st. as well as the first and last st. of the row.

11th row : Increase in every 17th st. as well as beginning and end.

13th row : As 11th row.

15th row : Increase in every 18th st. as well as the beginning and end.

Before cutting the cotton sew up the last 7 rows, then slip-stitch along one row and make 3 loops on one edge as described on the collar, and 3 buttons opposite to match.

Work a second cuff in the same way.

* * *

LOOK OUT FOR MORE FASCINATING WOOLLIES IN OUR NEXT NUMBER

A NEW NOTION IN JUMPERS

(Continued from the facing page)

The Diagram of the Jumper

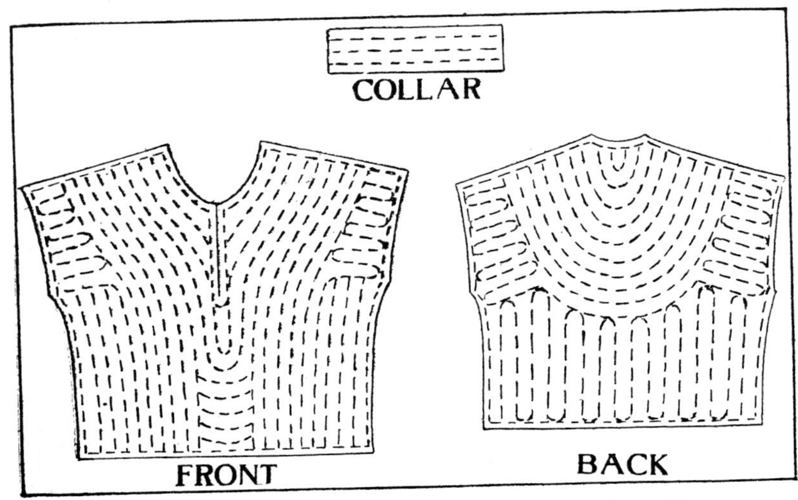

The dotted lines indicate the strips of treble crochet. You can adapt this to your pattern.

Fill this with trebles, and continue the tacking down according to the pattern.

Continue in this way until the lines of the design are all covered.

Join all the braids together with faggot-stitching (see diagram below). Remove from the brown paper and press. Then join up the blouse seams in the ordinary way, by hand.

The collar is made of three strips of the crochet joined together with faggoting in the same way.

A chiffon lining cut from the same paper pattern is an improvement, as the blouse does not want to be too transparent.

Remember to allow for turnings when cutting The original jumper illustrated is fastened with 12 pearl buttons and loops.

Work diagonal faggoting from right to left.

Draw the needle point downwards through the top edge with the thread under the point. Then insert it point upwards through the lower edge in the same way (the thread under the point), but a little to the left.

Continue in this way to get a herring-bone effect.

A New Notion For Jumpers

Strips of Simple Treble Crochet are Joined Together with Faggoting

You can adapt any Magyar pattern to this kind of work.

This attractive jumper is entirely composed of strips of crochet joined by faggoting.

A simple pattern of back and front must first be cut in brown paper (see diagrams on facing page. Shape this from a blouse which fits you well. Then you make a length of crochet, as described below, and begin tacking it to the brown paper, as the lines on the diagram indicate.

Materials

For a blouse measuring 38 inches round the bust and 21 inches long from the shoulder, 4 ounces of Greenock 3-ply Super-fingering wool (obtainable at any of the branches of the Scotch Wool & Hosiery Stores) and a No. 10 hook (for trebles half an inch high) ; some small skeins of Anchor stranded cotton, biscuit colour as a contrast with any gaily coloured wool, for the faggoting.

To Work

First cut a paper pattern the shape you require in brown paper. Now, with the wool and crochet hook, work about 3 yards of crochet chain, and proceed to fill it with trebles, thus . 1 tr. into the 4th ch. from the hook, 1 tr. into each st. to the end of the ch. (Do not break off the wool.)

Take *the beginning* of this strip, and tack down to the paper pattern following the lines of the design. Tack along the centre of the crochet strip, and when within a few inches of the end, join a fresh length of wool to the last chain of the foundation, and work a further length of chain.

(continued, p. 14)

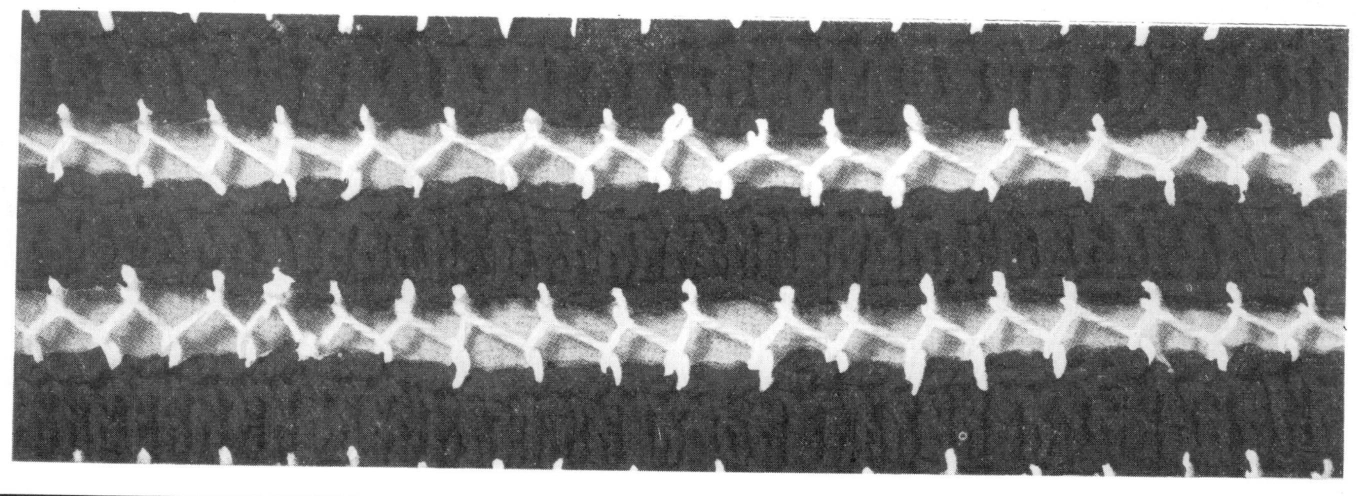

"Listening-

NO INTRICATE PATTE
OR TALK AND BE S

No. 1 JUMPER

This is the jumper that you can work if you only know how to make a treble and chain-stitch, as shown on page 4. The open treble groups make a very lacy pattern, particularly in the new, fine crochet silk.

MATERIALS

Use 8 oz. of Rickards' Medium Artificial Silk, which is about half the thickness of the ordinary art silk. This quantity makes a small jumper for a figure 32 to 34 inches bust measure, as shown on diagram, the latter allowing 4 inches over actual measurement of wearer. Less than ½ oz. more is required, so odd lengths of a contrasting colour would make the roses and edging. Use a No. 1 Roma steel crochet hook.

BEGIN AT BACK

Make 154 ch.

1st row : 1 tr. in seventh ch. from hook, * miss 2 ch., 1 tr., 2 ch., 1 tr. in next stitch, and repeat from * to end. Turn, without chain.

2nd row : S.s. into first ch. after tr. 5 ch., 1 tr. in first sp., then 1 tr., 2 ch., 1 tr. into each sp. of 2 ch. between trs. Turn.

Repeat 2nd row 14 times, then increase 1 sp. at the beginning and end of every row until the measurement required up to underarm seam is attained. In the model illustrated there are 28 rows. To increase work an extra 2 ch. and 1 tr. into last sp. of 2 ch., between trebles. At end of this row, add 54 ch., and fasten off securely. Rejoin the silk to the first stitch of the last row worked and make 61 ch. Turn and work as first row and go right across all the stitches to end of chain on opposite sleeve. Work 17 more rows to bring work up to the back of neck.

Count the number of groups and mark the centre, count eight groups each side of this to leave free for back of neck, and mark each eighth group with a piece of white cotton so that it will not be worked into.

Now work up to the first mark for one shoulder for 19 rows. Work the other shoulder to correspond, beginning at sleeve end so that the last row will finish at neck end, where add 51 ch. and s.s. to end stitch on opposite side of neck and fasten off.

Rejoin silk at end of sleeve and work right across from one end of sleeve to the other for three more rows, and fasten off. On the next row leave 18 groups free at end of sleeve, and join silk in next group and work across front to corresponding group on second sleeve, leaving 18 groups free this end. Now work down front, decreasing 1 sp. each end for as many rows as were increased on back, and then continue down to waist for same number of rows as back. Fasten off.

THE BASQUES

These are worked in two parts.

Make 135 ch. and work like body of jumper for 10 rows.

These bands are sewn on, the centre of jumper being slightly gathered at back and front.

Sew up underarm and sleeve seams.

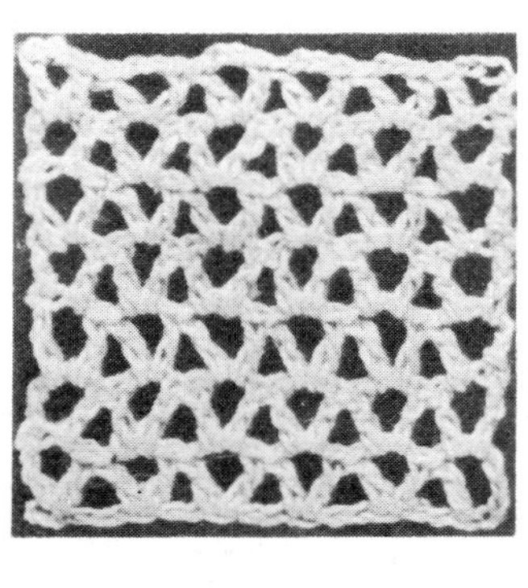

An open, lacy pattern of trebles and chains.

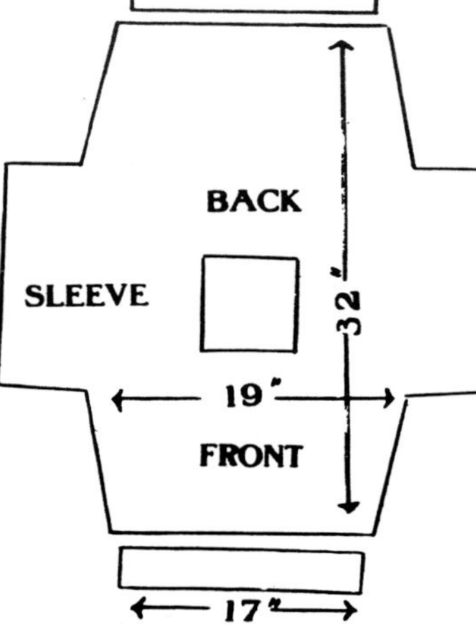

ROSES FOR BANDS

Six of these are worked separately and three sewn on each band.

Make 6 ch. and join into a ring with a s.s., 1 d.c., 3 tr., 1 d.c. four times into ring, work 4 ch. at back of each petal, putting a d.c. between the petals to hold down the chain loops. Into each fourth ch. sp. put 1 d.c., 5 tr., 1 d.c., and fasten off.

EDGING FOR NECK AND SLEEVES

1 d.c., 3 ch., 1 d.c. into each sp.

No. 2 JUMPER

This is worked in a very simple pattern of 1 sp. and block of tr. alternately. It is a very easy all-over design.

MATERIALS

Use 8 oz. of "Flossella" Wool as sold at Evans' Stores and a No. 1 steel crochet-hook.

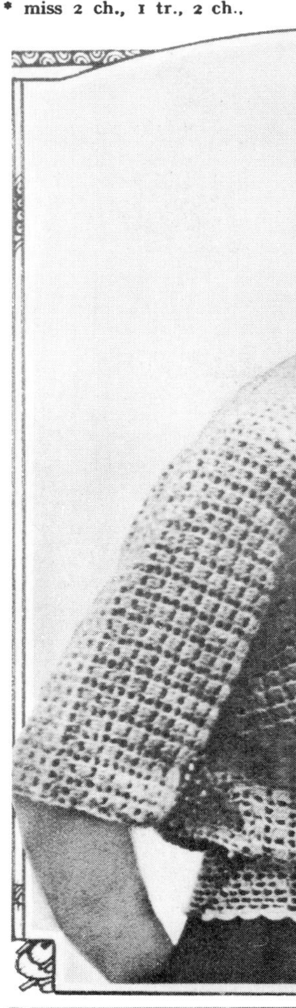

n" Jumpers

YOU CAN "LISTEN-IN"
BLE WHILE WORKING

SIZE AND TENSION

This jumper has quite a wide front, as the shoulder and short sleeve fall well over the arm, so the big figure that takes it up in the body can add a crochet lace to lengthen sleeve ; or it is a very simple matter to add extra chain when working the sleeve. This also applies to the beginning of the work, when every 6 ch. added will make 1 sp. and a block extra.

BEGIN AT BACK

Make 164 ch.

1st row : 1 tr. into eighth ch. from hook, * 2 ch., miss 2 ch., 1 tr. in next ch. making a sp., and repeat from * to end of row, 5 ch. Turn.

2nd row : 1 tr. on second tr., making the first sp. with the 5 turning ch., 2 tr. under 2 ch. and 1 tr. on next tr. making a block of 4 tr. with the tr. finishing the last sp., and continue the row in this manner, 1 sp. and 3 tr. alternately to end.

These two rows form the whole pattern, and must be repeated nine more times to bring the work up to the gusset. Now increase 1 sp. or block of tr. according to pattern at the beginning of each of the next 14 rows, or until it is long enough to reach the underarm. The lines of blocks must be kept straight over each other, so watch this after increasing.

The increase is made thus : 6 ch., 1 tr. on the very first tr., instead of missing this as in previous rows. When you return to this point at the end of next row you must work into this ch. sp. If the pattern brings a sp. here, make 2 ch., miss 2 ch., 1 tr. into the third tr. of this loop. If it ends with a block, work 1 tr. into each of the first 3 ch. of the loop, making 4 tr. with the one finishing the last sp.

THE SLEEVES

At the beginning of each of the next two rows add 53 ch. for sleeves, work 22 more rows of pattern across all these stitches to bring the work up to back of neck.

THE FRONT

Work 22 rows of pattern on 45 sp. only, and fasten off the wool.

Work the second front in the same way, beginning at the neck end so that you will finish at the neck end. Here do 32 ch. and s.s. this ch. to the corresponding corner on first front at neck. Join the wool to the end of the 16th sp. from sleeve end. This will leave 16 sp. (or 8 sp. and 8 blocks) free for the sleeve.

Work in pattern across the row up to within 16 sp. of opposite end of sleeve. Now continue in pattern like the back, but decreasing 1 sp. at the underarm at the beginning of each of the next 14 rows. These decreasings correspond with the increasings of the back, and form the front gusset.

To decrease, work 3 ch. only, then 1 tr. on second tr., and when you come to the end of the next row do not work under these 3 ch.

Now continue to waist of jumper, working exactly the same number of rows as on back. Sew up the side and underarm seams.

THE BASQUE

Beginning at a side seam, work 1 tr. in each stitch all round jumper, except at centre front, where work into every other stitch to give a little fullness to the top. Turn with 5 ch. when you reach the side seam at which you commenced.

Continue in rows of pattern like body of jumper until the basque is the depth required (14 rows on model), and finish with a row of shells, putting 5 tr. in 1 sp. and 1 d.c. in the next.

Sew up the two ends of basque at side seam.

The neck has a little picot edging, or it can be finished with shells like the basque.

For the picot edge work thus : * 1 d.c. in a space, 4 ch., s.s. into

THIS JUMPER COST LESS THAN FOUR SHILLINGS TO MAKE

BACK
17"
34"
SLEEVE
26"
FRONT
5½"

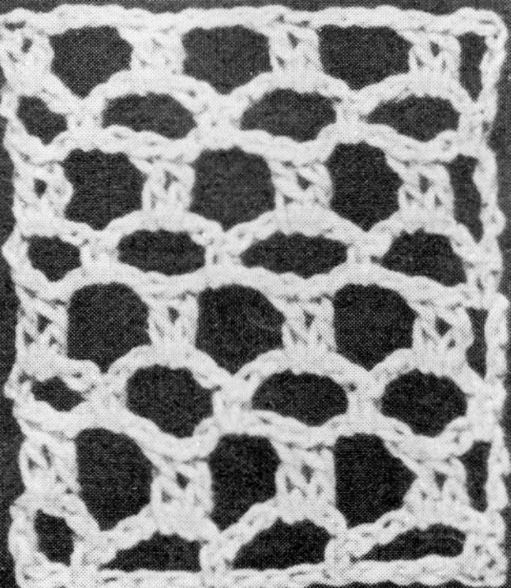

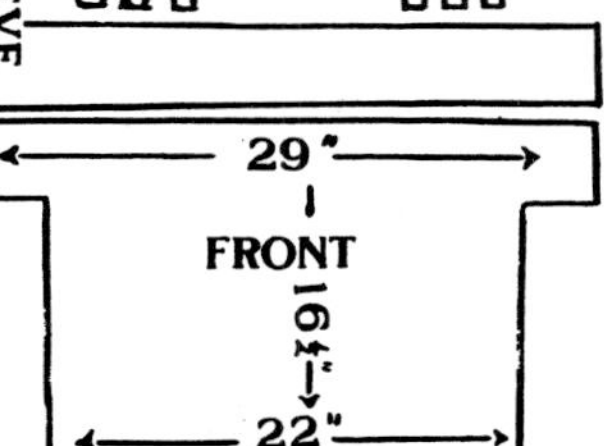

This Jumper is worked across the front, instead of up, so you can work as many rows as required for a full figure.

"Listening-In" Jumpers

the fourth ch. from hook to form a picot, 1 d.c. in same space, 1 d.c. in next space, and repeat from * all round.

No. 3 JUMPER

This might be called the "easiest-of-all" jumper, as far as construction is concerned, and it is so amenable to alteration to suit one's own requirements. The original was worked in knitting cotton for a summer sports jumper; or worked in an artificial silk, it would make a simple party garment, as the two pieces are connected with shoulder-straps.

MATERIALS

Five 2 oz. balls of Strutt's Milford Knitting Cotton No. 8 (two of cream, three of pink, or any other colour) and a steel crochet-hook, No. 0.

SIZE

The above quantities will make a jumper for a 34 to 38 inches bust measure with short sleeves, but these can be made any length, or a crochet lace pattern can be added. The work proceeds across the front from one side to the other, so as many rows as required can be continued.

This could be worked in two pieces only—back and front—but if using two colours it is easier to make a yoke of one colour by working a length of insertion and sew to body of jumper afterwards.

ABBREVIATIONS

Ch., chain; d.c., double crochet; tr., treble; sp., space; lacet consists of 3 ch., miss 2 st., 1 d.c. into next, 3 ch., miss 2 st., 1 tr. into next; bar, usually worked over a lacet, and consisting of 5 ch., 1 tr. on tr. at end of lacet; s.s., slip-stitch; st., stitch.

Begin with insertion, using cream cotton.

Make 43 ch.

1st row: 1 tr. into fourth ch. from hook, 1 tr. into each of the next 3 ch., * 1 lacet, 3 tr.,; repeat from * three times, 5 ch. Turn.

2nd row: Miss 3 tr., 1 tr. in next tr. forming sp., * 1 bar, 1 sp.; repeat from * three times, 3 ch. Turn.

3rd row: Miss first tr. over which 3 ch. stands, as this will represent 1 tr., * 3 tr., 1 lacet, 1 tuft, 1 lacet; repeat from *, 5 ch. Turn.

4th row: Same as 2nd row.

5th row: 3 tr., 1 lacet, 3 tr., 1 lacet, 1 tuft (1 lacet and 3 tr.), twice, 5 ch. Turn.

6th row: Same as 2nd row.

7th row: Same as 3rd row.

The 2nd, 3rd, 4th, and 5th rows now constitute the pattern.

Continue for a length of 29 inches, or according to width of jumper required.

FRONT AND BACK

Worked in coloured cotton, two pieces exactly alike. The pattern consists of two rows only. Small sleeve piece is worked first.

Begin at left-hand corner with 21 ch.

1st row: 1 d.c. in eighth ch. from hook, * 5 ch., miss 3 ch., 1 d.c. in next; repeat from * twice, and turn with 5 ch.

2nd row: 2 tr. under first loop of 5 ch., * 3 ch., 2 tr. in next loop; repeat from * twice. Turn with 5 ch.

The next row is like the first, only 1 d.c. is worked under loop of 3 ch. Repeat the two rows until there are 11 rows altogether. At the end of 11th row work 117 ch., which represents the length of the side seam. Turn and work 1 tr. into eighth ch. from hook, 1 tr. in next st., * 3 ch., miss 2 ch., 1 tr. in each of next 2 st., and repeat from * across all ch., and into loops on short row.

Repeat the two pattern rows until the piece measures 22 inches from side seam, then work the short piece only for second sleeve, and fasten off.

EDGING FOR HEM OF JUMPER

In cream, work 18 ch.

1st row: 1 tr. into fourth ch, 6 more to form a tuft, then 5 ch., miss 5 ch., 1 tr. into next ch., forming a bar, 1 lacet, 3 tr., 5 ch. Turn.

2nd row: 1 tr. on fourth tr., 1 bar, 9 ch. Turn.

Repeat these two rows until long enough to fit hem of jumper.

The sleeve edging consists of 1 d.c. in each stitch round edge, or a piece to match hem can be sewn on.

SHOULDER-STRAPS

These are set at equal distances, three on each shoulder, the longest one nearest the neck.

Make 12 ch., 1 tr. into fourth ch. from hook, then 1 tr. in each stitch to end of row, 3 ch. Turn.

Work seven more rows of trebles for this strap.

The second strap has 6 rows and the third strap 4 rows.

At end of sleeve join the two cream insertions for three blocks along, or a distance of about 2 inches.

THE GIRDLE

This is worked in two colours.

Wind cotton five or six times round forefinger and middle finger of left hand loosely, then crochet 23 d.c. round ring, make a second ring and join to previous one, when it is half filled with d.c., by slip-stitching to corresponding stitch on first ring. The girdle illustrated has 20 rings, but it can be made any length to suit wearer.

Now work in cream an edging all round as follows: 1 d.c., * 5 ch., miss 3 d.c. on ring, 1 d.c., 5 ch., miss 3 d.c., 1 d.c. in next st., 2 ch., 1 tr. in between 2 rings, 2 ch., miss 2 d.c. on next ring, 1 d.c. in next; repeat from *. This is worked all round so that there are cream loops on each side of rings.

The end of girdle has a rose attached, worked like the rose on No. 1 Jumper on page 8. The one illustrated has four rounds of petals, but some may prefer only two rounds. The petals have d.c. worked in white all round them.

Before sewing ornament to girdle, work a little tape of four rows of 4 tr. on each end of the girdle. Sew the ornament on to this on the one end, and underneath a press-stud. On the other side sew the other portion of the press-stud.

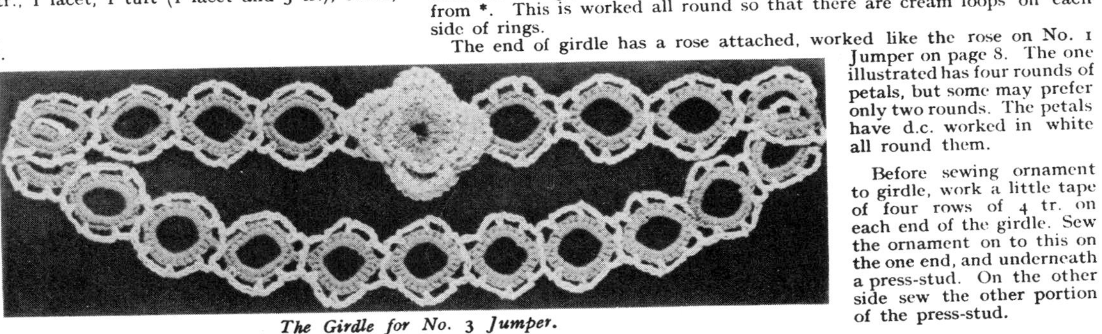

The Girdle for No. 3 Jumper.

How to Make TUFTS LACETS AND BARS AS USED ON No. 3 Jumper

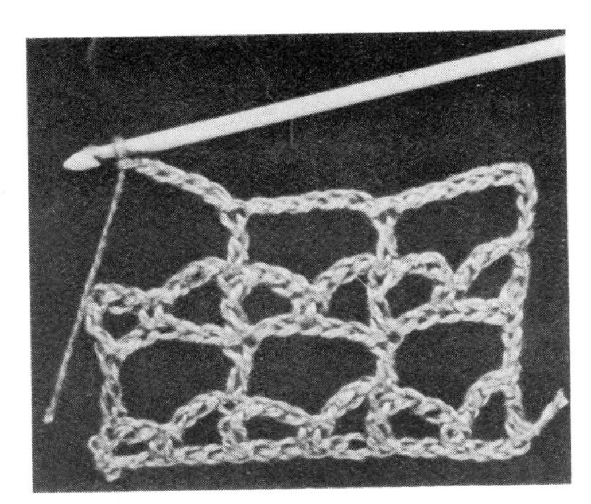

MAKING A TUFT

This tuft is worked into a space, that is, *under* the 2 ch., not into it. After working the treble on treble to complete the last space, work 5 tr. under the next space. Now take hook out of last stitch, put it in top of first of these 5 tr., then catch the loop just dropped at top of fifth treble, and draw it through first loop. Make one firm chain-stitch to lock the tuft, then 1 tr. on tr. after the space.

LACETS AND BARS

A lacet is 3 ch., miss 2 stitches, 1 d.c. in the next stitch (or in centre of bar), then 3 ch., miss 2 stitches, 1 tr. in the next stitch. A bar is 5 ch., miss the 2 loops of 3 ch. of lacet (or miss 5 stitches), then 1 tr. on the next tr.

The above illustration shows bars worked over lacets.

CROCHET BEADS

No. An. 9.

DO you want a new idea for Christmas gifts? Well, here you are—a link of beads with a bracelet to match, crocheted in Strutt's Macramé Twine!

The long beads are made with Strutt's Macramé Twine No. 10, shade 702 variegated orange and brown, of which you will require one 2-oz. ball, also one 2-oz. ball of shade 526 bright green, and two necklace clasps. Use a No. 1 Milward's steel hook.

Commence with 5 chain (ch.) Join to the first loop to form a ring.

1st round. Do not work tightly; a little practice will enable you to make a bead perfectly.

1 double crochet (d.c.) into each ch., lifting the back loop. (Keep the end of the Macramé inside when working.)

Do not join each round with a slip stitch, but work right on with d.c., lifting the small stitch at the back between the d.c. of the last round. The back of the stitches forms the outside of the bead. The row you have just completed falls inside the bead and acts as a padding.

Continue like this until the required length is obtained, about 1 in., then work slip stitch for the last round instead of d.c. Break off thread, leaving a length about 10 ins., and fasten neatly with a tapestry needle. Take the needle, with the thread, through the bead to the other end and fix.

When you have enough beads made (there are 16 in the original), thread them on to a thread of green Macramé, making a knot between the beads. Attach a clasp for fastening.

The bracelet is made in the same way, with 7 beads.

The Round Beads.—Materials required—one 2-oz. ball of Strutt's Macramé Twine No. 10, shade 708 variegated green, two necklace clasps.

Commence with 3 ch. Join to the first loop to form a ring.

1st round. 1 d.c. into each ch., lifting the back loop.

Work as for the long bead for about 3 rounds, then slip stitch all round instead of d.c. and fix neatly as above.

The instructions are given for the smallest beads and the size gradually increases towards the centre. To make the larger ones, commence with more ch. and work more rows of d.c.

Thread the beads on to a piece of green twine, without knotting them. There are 41 beads in all. Attach a clasp for fastening.

Make the bracelet in the same way, with 19 beads.

The Fashionable

"STRING" EFFECT

CREATED WITH

Ardern's White Crochet Cotton.

THE LATEST EFFECT.

Achieved with White Crochet Cotton.

COARSE White crochet cotton gives this Jumper blouse a decidedly Parisian air, and makes it so smart for wear with a summer tailor made. Use 9 balls of Ardern's White Crochet, size 6, and a medium steel hook.

Width round underarm = 34 inches. Length from shoulder = 18 inches.

The front and the back are worked downwards from the yoke line.

Abbreviations:

Ch., chain; tr., treble; l.tr., long treble; d.c., double crochet.

FRONT.

161 ch., the last 3 ch to stand for 1st tr. in 1st row.

1st row. 78 tr., 5 tr. into centre ch., 79 tr..

2nd row. 1 tr. into each stitch of previous row with 5 tr. into centre stitch. Work into front of each treble.

3rd row. 3 ch. 1 d.c. into 2nd tr., * 2 ch. miss 1 tr., 1 d.c. in next, repeat from *, putting 2 ch. and 1 d.c. twice into centre treble.

4th and 5th rows. As the 3rd.

6th row. As the last but working 1 ch. instead of 2 ch. along the row.

Repeat these 6 rows 3 times. Then repeat them again twice and the 1st and 2nd rows once more, decreasing 2 tr. at each end of the 1st and 2nd rows and 1 ch. loop at each end of the 3rd to 6th rows. The centre point at the lower edge of front of Jumper is now reached and the left and right hand corners are finished one at a time. Work each in pattern for 22 rows decreasing at each end of the row instead of at the underarm edge only.

The back is worked as for the front but commencing with 131 ch.; 63 tr., 5 tr. into centre ch., 64 tr..

SLEEVES (both alike). 54 ch..

Work the six pattern rows three times omitting the increase in the centre of the row but increasing at each end of every row (2 tr. at each end of tr. rows and 1 ch. loop at each end on remaining rows).

Join the beginning of last row to the end and work round for 8 rows in pattern (to avoid a seam). Sew up side seams, also first 18 rows of the sleeve to the corresponding rows of back and front of Jumper.

Around the lower edge work rows 1 to 5 of pattern, decreasing at the seam and increasing slightly to turn the corners.

YOKE.

The lace like yoke is worked separately and made entirely of rows of Solomon's knots. This stitch is made as follows:—

* Draw out the loop on the hook to the length of 2 ch. thread over hook and draw through loop, then work a d.c. into the single loop behind * and repeat to complete. For a half knot work only from * to *.

Commence at lower point of centre back by making 2 knots. Join with a slip stitch.

2nd row. Work one and a half knots, 1 d.c. into centre d.c. of knot below, one and a half knots 1 d.c. between the 2 knots of 1st row, slip stitch along the last half knot made.

3rd row. 1 and a half knots, 1 d.c. into centre of knot below, 1 knot. 1 d.c. into centre of next knot below, 1 and a half knots, 1 d.c. into end of same knot, slip stitch along last half knot made.

4th row. 1 and a half knots, proceed in the same manner as for previous rows. It will be seen that each row increases by one knot and the work should be continued to form a triangular shape, until there are 26 knots in the row (26 rows). Break off thread.

Now commence front of yoke in a similar manner and work until there are 21 knots in the row.

22nd row. Continue as for preceding rows until 9 knots have been worked, slip stitch along the last half knot, turn the work and continue on these stitches for one shoulder.

23rd row. 8 knots, 1 and a half knots, 1 d.c. into next d.c. below, slip stitch along the last half knot. Work until the 27th row has been completed, increasing on the armhole edge and decreasing at the neck edge in this way, keeping 9 knots in the row. At the end of the 27th row slip stitch up 1 whole knot instead of a half knot as previously.

28th row. 8 knots.

29th row. Decreasing at neck edge as usual, make 7 knots, then 1 and a half knots, slip stitching back along 1 whole knot as at end of 27th row.

30th row. 7 knots, slip stitch along last half knot.

31st row. As the 29th but making 6 knots and ending the row similarly.

32nd row. 6 knots.

33rd row. 1 and a half knots, 1 d.c. into next d.c., 5 knots, 1 and a half knots, 1 d.c. into next d.c., slip stitch back along 1 whole knot.

Repeat the last two rows alternately until the 45th row has been worked.

46th row. 6 knots, 1 and a half knots, 1 d.c. into next d.c. below, slip stitch along a half knot.

47th row. 1 and a half knots, 1 d.c. into next d.c. below, 6 knots, 1 and a half knots, 1 d.c. into next d.c. below, slip stitch along 1 whole knot.

48th row. 7 knots, 1 and a half knots, 1 d.c. into next d.c., slip stitch along last half knot.

49th row. 1 and a half knots, 1 d.c. into next d.c., 7 knots.

50th row. 1 and a half knots, 1 d.c. into next d.c., 7 knots, 1 and a half knots, 1 d.c. into next d.c., slip stitch along one half knot.

51st row. 1 and a half knots, 1 d.c. into next d.c., 8 knots.

Break off thread and join at commencement of 21st row, reversing 22nd to 51st rows for second side of neck. When this is completed slip stitch the shoulders to the back portion, leaving 6 knots in the centre to form back of neckline.

Set the yoke into the Jumper easing in any extra fulness over the shoulders. Next crochet a row of d.c. round the neck edge.

To work the edging at the neck, commence with * a group of 3 l.tr., working the last stitches off together; miss 2 d.c. and work another group of 3 l.tr. into next stitch. * 3 ch., 2 l.tr. into top of first group below, working last of the l.tr. stitches off with the 3rd ch. stitch; 2 ch., one group of 3 l.tr. into top of second group below.

* * 7 ch., miss 5 d.c. of neck edge and work from * to * 3 ch., slip stitch to 4th of seven ch. and work 1 l.tr. into top of 1st group below; 2 ch., 1 group into top of 2nd group below * *, repeat from * * to * * round neck. Finish with a row of d.c..

For the tie work 7 rows of Solomon's knots as for commencement of yoke to form a triangular piece. Make another triangle and join the two together at the end of the last lines. Finish the ends of the tie with 2 rows of treble crochet and slot through border at neck edge.

FASHION HONOURS HER CHECKS

crochet this double-breasted coat and darn in the check pattern

THIS double-breasted coat-jumper will be useful both at the present time, for slipping on over thin frocks, and in the autumn, for wearing as an ordinary jumper. It is crocheted in an open lattice pattern, which is then darned to give the checked effect. The original is in two shades of green.

●

MATERIALS: Of "Beehive" (or Paton's Super) Scotch Fingering, 3-ply, 4 ozs. in dark green, shade 2031, and 4 ozs. in light green, shade 600. A pair No. 10 "Inox" knitting needles; a No. 8 "Inox" crochet hook; a tapestry needle. Four steel buttons.

MEASUREMENTS: Length, 17 inches; bust, 34 inches; sleeve seam, 18 inches.

TENSION: 7 blocks of treble—2 inches in width.

THE FRONTS

With dark green wool, cast on 64 stitches. Work 28 rows in k. 1, p. 1 ribbing. Cast off loosely and fasten off wool.

Join light green wool into first stitch, and work first row of the crochet into the cast-off stitches. 1ST ROW: 4 ch., * miss 1, 1 tr. into next, 1 ch., repeat from *, ending with 1 tr. into last stitch (32 treble in all, counting the ch. at beginning which stand for first treble). 2ND ROW: Turn with 4 ch., 1 tr. on next tr., * 1 ch., 1 tr. on next tr., repeat from * to end. Change to dark green and repeat 2nd row twice.

The whole of the garment is worked in this pattern, 2 rows in each colour. When 18 rows have been done in all (or more if coat is preferred longer), shape for armhole by missing 1 tr. at one edge (keeping the other edge straight), in the next and every alternate row, four times in all. Work without further decreasing until the 37th row, when the shoulder shaping begins. Miss 2 tr. at the armhole edge in every alternate row, four times. Break off.

Work the other front exactly the same.

THE BACK

With No. 10 needles and dark green wool, cast on 88 stitches. Work in ribbing of k. 1, p. 1 for 28 rows. Cast off loosely. With light green wool, work pattern exactly as for front (44 tr. in 1st row).

When 18 rows have been done, shape for armhole by missing 1 tr. at each end of the next and every alternate row, four times. Work without further decreasing until 36 rows have been done. Shape for shoulders by missing 2 tr. at the end of the next 8 rows. Break off.

THE SLEEVES

With No. 10 needles and dark green wool, cast on 50 stitches. Work in ribbing of k. 1, p. 1 for 28 rows. Cast off loosely. With crochet hook and light green wool, work same pattern as for back and front (25 tr. in row).

Increase in the 8th and 9th and every subsequent 8th and 9th rows, by turning with 5 ch. and making 1 tr. on the 1st instead of the 2nd tr. Increase until there are 35 tr. in all, then work on these until 50 rows have been done. Shape for top of sleeve by missing 1 tr. at end of next 4 rows, then miss 2 tr. at the end of the next 4 rows. Break off.

THE DARNING

First press all pieces very carefully with damp cloth and hot iron, pulling out to the right dimensions.

The darning is done with double wool, starting at the bottom and working to the top and back in each vertical line of holes. Fill in two lines with one colour, the next two with the other colour; this gives the checked effect. Leave the ends of wool loose.

The darning finished again, press the pieces carefully. Tie the loose ends of wool together and run in the ends neatly.

Sew side, shoulder and sleeve seams, and insert sleeves. Stitch four buttons to left front. Make corresponding buttonholes in right front by pushing a pencil through the darning to make a hole and buttonholing round this.

● Two shades of green are used for this attractive little coat jumper. It is double breasted, with fairly wide revers. The check pattern is achieved by darning on a crochet foundation.

OFF TO BRIDGE IN A DASHING SUIT

SHE'S ready for an afternoon's bridge, wearing a perfectly fitting suit crocheted in a yarn with a lovely silky feel. You can make this quite easily, too; but we don't deny it takes time.

●

MATERIALS: 37 skeins of Pearsall's "Pamela" Sparkle twist. Original uses copper beech shade. A No. 12 and a No. 13 "Inox" crochet hook. A zip-fastener. One large button and petersham for waistband. Two large hooks and eyes.

MEASUREMENTS: Coat: to fit 34–36-inch bust; length from top of shoulder, 21½ inches; sleeve seam, 5 inches.

Skirt: waist, 26–28 inches; hips, 36–38 inches; length, 30 inches.

TENSION: Coat, 7 stitches to an inch; skirt, 6 stitches to an inch.

ABBREVIATIONS: ch.=chain; d.c.=double crochet; tr.=treble.

COAT

Use the No. 13 hook throughout the coat, turn always at the end of each row with 1 ch.

BACK

Make 115 ch. 1ST ROW: 1 d.c. into 2nd ch. from hook and into each ch. to end of row. Work 5 more rows of d.c., decreasing 1 stitch at beginning of 3rd and 4th rows. 7TH ROW: 1 d.c. into 1st d.c., * 1 tr. into each of next 2 d.c., 1 d.c. into each of next 2 d.c. Repeat from * to last 3 stitches, 2 tr., 1 d.c.

8TH ROW: Decrease 1 stitch at each end of row, and work 1 tr. in each d.c. and 1 d.c. in each tr. of previous row. Working thus, 2 d.c. and 2 tr. alternately one above the other, forms the pattern, which is used throughout the suit.

Continue in pattern, decreasing 1 stitch at each end of every following 4th row until 36 rows have been done.

There should now be 96 stitches on the row. Work 6 rows straight.

Now increase 1 stitch (by working 2 stitches in the first and last stitches of the row) at each end of next and every following 5th row until there are 108 stitches in a row. Work 4 rows straight.

Shape for armholes thus:—Decrease 4 stitches at each end of next row, then 1 stitch at each end of next 8 rows (84 stitches now in the row). Work 25 rows straight, then shape shoulders by missing 3 stitches at each end of next 8 rows. 9TH ROW: Miss 2 stitches at each end. 10TH ROW: Work 1 d.c. in each stitch of last row. Work 5 more rows of d.c., decreasing 1 stitch at beginning of each row. Fasten off.

LEFT FRONT

Make 53 ch. 1ST ROW: 1 d.c. into 2nd ch. from hook, * 1 tr. in each of next 2 ch., 1 d.c. in each of next 2 ch. Repeat from * to last 3 stitches, 2 tr., 1 d.c. 2ND ROW: Increase 1 stitch, work in pattern to end. 3RD ROW: Work in pattern without increase. Repeat 2nd and 3rd rows twice more. Work 7 rows straight.

15TH ROW: Decrease 1 stitch at beginning of row, 12 stitches in pattern, ch. 24, miss 24 stitches of last row, 1 tr. in next stitch, in pattern to end. 16TH ROW: Work in pattern, and continue 2 tr., 2 d.c. along the 24 ch. Finish row in pattern. Work 3 rows straight.

20TH ROW: Decrease 1 stitch at end of row. Work 4 rows straight. 25TH ROW: Decrease 1 stitch at beginning of row, in pattern to end. 26TH ROW: Now start to shape rever by increasing 1 stitch at beginning of row; in pattern to end. 27TH ROW: Work in pattern. 28TH ROW: Increase 1 stitch at rever edge; in pattern to end. 29TH ROW: As 27th. 30TH ROW: Increase 1 stitch at beginning and decrease 1 stitch at end of row.

**Continue to increase 1 stitch at every alternate row at front edge and keep armhole edge straight for 6 more rows. Then, still increasing as before at front edge, increase 1 stitch at next and every following 5th row at under-arm edge until there are 76 stitches on a row.

Work 4 rows straight. Continue as follows:—1ST ROW: Decrease 4 stitches at armhole edge. 2ND ROW: Increase 1 stitch at front edge and decrease 1 stitch at armhole edge. 3RD ROW: Decrease 1 stitch at armhole edge. 4TH ROW: Increase 1 stitch at front edge, pattern for 40 stitches, ch. 18, miss 18 stitches of last row, pattern for 11 stitches, turn. 5TH ROW: Decrease 1 stitch at armhole edge; work to end in pattern, working over the 18 ch.

On next 5 rows continue to increase at front edge, and decrease 1 stitch in every row at armhole edge. Now work 6 rows straight. 17TH ROW: Decrease 2 stitches at front edge. 18TH ROW: Decrease 1 stitch at front edge. Repeat last 2 rows until there are 40 stitches on the row.

Now shape shoulders by decreasing 3 stitches at armhole edge on next 8 rows, still decreasing as before at front edge. 9TH ROW: Miss 1 stitch, 2 d.c. Fasten off.

Work 6 rows of d.c. from the shoulder, along the front edge, and across lower edge to under-arm edge. When turning a corner, work 2 d.c. in the corner stitch.

Work a border of 6 rows of d.c. across lower edge of large pocket slit and 4 rows across lower edge of small pocket. Make pocket linings by working 9 rows of tr. across top edge of slit of large pocket, with 5 rows for the small pocket.

RIGHT FRONT

Make 53 ch. 1ST ROW: As 1st row of left front. 2ND ROW: Work in pattern, increase 1 stitch at end of row. 3RD ROW: In pattern. Repeat 2nd and 3rd rows twice more. Work 7 rows straight.

15TH ROW: 18 stitches in pattern, ch. 24, miss 24 stitches of last row, pattern for 12 stitches, turn. NEXT 4 ROWS: In pattern. 20TH ROW: Decrease 1 stitch at beginning of row. Work 3 rows straight. 25TH ROW: Decrease 1 stitch at end of row.

26TH ROW: In pattern to last 6 stitches. Make a buttonhole as follows:—ch. 5, miss 5 stitches of last row, 1 d.c., 1 tr. in last stitch. This increase begins the rever.

27TH ROW: Work straight. 28TH ROW: Increase 1 stitch at front edge. 29TH ROW: Work straight. 30TH ROW: Decrease 1 stitch at beginning and increase 1 stitch at end of row. Now work as from ** of left front, but omit the small pocket in 70th row, which is worked thus:—Decrease 1 stitch at armhole and increase 1 stitch at front edge.

SLEEVES

Make 65 ch. 1ST ROW: As 1st row of left front. Work in pattern, increasing 1 stitch at each end of 2nd and every following 3rd row until 20 rows have been done.

Shape top by decreasing 2 stitches at each end of next 5 rows, then decrease 1 stitch at each end of every row until 18 remain. Fasten off.

Work 6 rows of d.c. along lower edge. Make a second sleeve in the same way.

SKIRT

BACK. Use the No. 12 hook throughout the skirt.

Start at lower edge with 117 ch. 1ST ROW: As 1st row of left front of coat. Work straight in pattern until work measures 19½ inches from lower edge for a 30-inch length skirt, but if you wish to make it longer, then work rather more rows at this point. Decrease 1 stitch at each end of next and every following 4th row, until there are 90 stitches in the row. Fasten off.

FRONT PANEL

Make 69 ch. 1ST ROW: As 1st row of left front of coat. Work straight in pattern for 12 inches. NEXT ROW: Miss 13 stitches at beginning of row, work in pattern on the next 42, turn. Work straight on these 42 for 18 inches. Any alteration in length should be made here. Fasten off.

RIGHT PANEL

Make 51 ch. 1ST ROW: 1 d.c. in 2nd ch. from hook, * 1 tr. in each of next 2 ch., 1 d.c. in each of next 2 ch.

(jumper, continued from p. 27)

Work back along this row to within 10 spaces of the top, turn (this begins the neck shaping). * Work to lower edge, then work back to top, omitting the last space. Repeat from * once, then work 2 rows in red, omitting the last space at the top. Repeat the 6 rows white and 2 red, still decreasing at top edge in alternate rows, then work straight, 6 rows white, 2 red, 3 white.

NEXT ROW: Work over 56 spaces only, then make a length of 43 ch. for other side of neck opening; work back over these ch. and on to lower edge. Work back to top edge.

Work 2 rows red, 6 white, without increasing, then * 2 rows red, 6 white, increasing in alternate rows at neck edge; repeat from * once. Make 22 ch. in white, then join in red and work over 53 spaces; turn, work back. Work 6 rows white, 2 red, 6 white.

* Next, work 2 rows red, decreasing at top edge in the 2nd row, then 6 rows white (no decrease); repeat from * twice. Break off white wool; join in red in 27th space from top. Work 2 rows red, 6 white, decreasing in alternate rows at armhole edge, then work 2 rows red, 6 white, 2 red, without decreasing. Break off.

SIDE PANELS

Sew up under-arm seams. With white wool work a row of pattern, flat along the lower edge of vertical stripes, join one panel extension to the other, across the side seam. In the original (1 d.c., 1 ch.) was worked 54 times in to this edge. Work (2 rows red, 6 white) 10 times, then 2 rows red; break off. Work similarly on the other side. Neatly sew each of these panels to the sides of back and front panels. Work 6 rows in white all round lower edge.

SLEEVES

With white wool, make a length of 63 ch. Work 6 rows white, and 2 red, then increase at top edge in alternate rows, until there are 6 red stripes. Work (6 white, 2 red) three times without increasing. Now decrease at same edge as previous increasing, in alternate rows, until 12 red and 12 white stripes have been worked from commencement. Work 2 red, 6 white and 2 red rows without shaping. Break off.

CUFFS

These are worked horizontally along lower edge of sleeves. Work (6 rows white, 2 red) twice; break off.

COLLAR

This is made in four similar pieces.

With white wool, make a length of 43 ch. Work in the striped pattern, 6 rows white, 2 red, for 22 rows, decreasing at outside edge in alternate rows. Work 3rd red stripe without decreasing; in the next white stripe begin increasing in alternate rows, and continue this increasing for 22 rows. Break off. Make three more pieces the same.

TO MAKE UP

Sew up shoulder and sleeve seams; sew in sleeves and turn back cuffs. Sew the four sections of collar to neck, overlapping them about the width of the first white stripe. Make loops of chain for buttonholes. Sew three buttons to each side of front opening.

OFF TO BRIDGE IN A DASHING SUIT

(continued from p. 25)

Now work straight in pattern for 12 inches. NEXT ROW: 37 stitches in pattern, turn, thus leaving 13 stitches for pleat on the inside edge.

**Work straight on these 37 stitches for 7½ inches. Any alteration in length should be made here. Decrease 1 stitch at the outside edge in next and every following 4th row, still working straight on the inside edge, until there are 24 stitches on the row. Fasten off.

LEFT PANEL

Work as for right panel for first 12 inches. NEXT ROW: Miss 13 stitches at beginning of row, work 37 in pattern. Now work as from ** of right panel.

TO MAKE UP

Press the pieces carefully under a damp cloth. For the coat, sew together side, shoulder and sleeve seams; insert sleeves. Stitch down pocket linings and sew down sides of pocket tops. Sew on button to match buttonhole.

To make up the skirt, join right and left panels to front panel. Turn the pleats under front panel to form a wide box pleat, and stitch along the top of each pleat. Tack them down and press under a damp cloth.

Join the back of skirt to the front, leaving an opening on the left side for the zipp-fastener. Stitch the petersham inside the top of skirt and fasten just under the zipp-fastener with hooks and eyes.

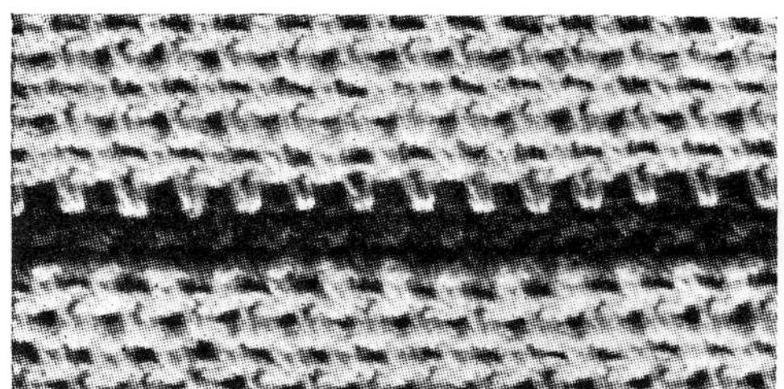

. . . OR WORK IT IN CROCHET

THE crochet version of the pin-striped jumper is seen on the cover, in a cherry and white colour-scheme which is charming for summer. Ordinary double crochet is used throughout, so there is nothing very complicated about the work. The little pointed collar (made from four exactly similar pieces) is an attractive little touch of frivolity!

●

MATERIALS: Of Paton's Super or "Beehive" Scotch Fingering, 2-ply, 5 ozs. in white, 2 ozs. in colour (original uses cherry, No. 2118). A No. 12 "Inox" crochet hook.

MEASUREMENTS: To fit bust 32 to 34 inches; length, 19½ inches; sleeve seam, 5½ inches.

TENSION: (1 d.c., 1 ch.) 5 times to 1 inch.

BACK

Begin at side seam with a length of 39 ch., using white wool.

1ST ROW: 1 d.c. in 3rd ch. from hook, * 1 ch., miss next stitch of foundation, 1 d.c. in next, repeat from * to end. 2ND ROW: Turn with 2 ch., 1 d.c. in 1st space, then (1 ch., 1 d.c.) in each space to end. Repeat 2nd row 4 times more.

7TH ROW: Join in red wool and work as 2nd row. 8TH ROW: As 2nd in red. 9TH ROW: White: Increase 1 stitch by turning with 3 ch. and working 1 d.c. into first of these, then continue (1 ch., 1 d.c.) in each space to end. 10TH ROW: As 2nd. Repeat last 2 rows twice more, then repeat them in red.

17TH ROW: White: Make 54 ch. for armhole and work back on this as the 1st row, then continue as 2nd row. Continue in pattern another 5 rows in white, then 2 in red.

* Increase (as previously explained) at beginning of next row (white) then work 5 more white rows, and 2 red rows. Repeat from * twice.**

Work next white row without an increase; at the end of it make 86 ch. This begins the centre panel of back. Continue in pattern, 6 rows white and 2 red, until there are 6 red stripes in the centre panel, then work 6 more rows in white, this completing centre panel. Change to red, work in pattern over 52 spaces, turn, work back in red.

* Work 6 rows in white, decreasing at end of 6th row by missing the last space. Work 2 rows in red, then repeat from * twice; work 6 rows in white. Break off white.

Join in red in the 27th space from top. Work 2 rows red, 6 rows white, decreasing in alternate rows at armhole edge, then work 2 rows red, 6 white and 2 red without decreasing. Break off.

FRONT

Work as for back as far as **, then work 6 rows white and 2 red without increasing. Work the next white row, then make 86 ch. for centre panel.

(continued on p. 26)

SWIM SUIT

THIS smart swim suit is so designed that on those gleaming hot days we all love so much it can be used for sunbathing too. The whole suit is crocheted, making it firm and cosy to wear.

MATERIALS

Baldwin and Walker's " Ladyship " holiday wool, 4-ply, 12 oz. terra cotta, 1 oz. dark green and 1 oz. white. A long tricot crochet hook, size 12, and two buttons.

ABBREVIATIONS.—Ch. chain, rep. repeat.

MEASUREMENTS

Size: 34. Bust (unstretched) 30 inches. Length of front (from neck to bottom of gusset) 26½ inches. Length of back 19 inches.

With the exception of the brassière top, for which separate stitch instructions will be given when necessary, the whole suit is made in Tunisian crochet, which is worked as follows:

1st row: * Insert hook into first ch., draw a loop through and leave it on the hook. Repeat from * to the end of ch. Twist the wool round the hook, pass it the first time through 1 loop, ** then twist the thread round the hook and draw it through 2 loops. Rep. from ** to end.

Working right to left and back again in this way counts as one row.

2nd row: Insert a hook into a vertical thread (not the one immediately under the hook, but the next), draw a loop through and leave it on the hook. * Insert the hook in the next vertical thread, draw a loop through and leave it on the hook. Rep. from * to left-hand edge of work. Work back as the second part of 1st row.

The 2nd row is repeated throughout.

To increase once at the beginning of the row, work 1 ch. and insert the hook in the end vertical thread of the row. To increase once at the opposite edge, draw a loop through the horizontal thread before the last vertical thread and then through the last vertical thread as usual.

To decrease at the beginning of the row, draw a loop through two vertical threads together. To decrease at the other edge, do not draw a loop through the last vertical thread.

FRONT

With terra-cotta wool make 2 ch.

1st row: As the first row given above.

2nd row: Increase once at the beginning and then work as the 2nd row above.

Rep. the 2nd row until there are 16 loops on the hook at the end of the first part of the 15th row. Do not work back on this row, but leave all the loops on the hook and break the wool.

Make another piece in the same way.

When the 16 loops have been made for the first part of the 15th row, work back along the row as usual, then pick up the first piece of work, join the broken end of wool to the wool in use and draw through all the loops on this piece to end of row.

16th row: Increase once at each edge.

Rep. the 16th row, until there are 46 stitches and 22 rows. *23rd row:* Work 2 ch. at the beginning, draw a loop through a ch., then through the vertical thread at the very end of the row. (Two increases.) Work along the row until there is 1 vertical thread left, draw a loop through one of the two horizontal threads, then through the other horizontal one, and finally through the vertical one as usual. Work back to end of row. *24th row:* Make 32 ch. Draw a loop through each of the chain and then through every vertical thread to the left-hand edge. Then make a separate length of 32 chain. Draw a loop through each of these chain, join to the crochet and work back to end of row as usual.

To make the suit larger or smaller make more or fewer chain. 7 ch. to 1 in. Work 20 rows without increasing.

Decrease once at each side of the next row.

Work 6 rows. Decrease once at each side of the next row. Work 3 rows. Work the last 4 rows twice more. Work 7 rows. Decrease once at each side of the next row. Work 4 rows. Decrease once at each side of the next row. Work 9 rows.

Decrease 2 at each side of the next row. (To decrease twice at the beginning, slip stitch along the top of the 2nd vertical thread and then work as usual. To decrease twice at the other side of the work, leave two vertical threads without drawing loops through them.)

Rep. the last row until there are 80 sts. left.

Decrease once at each side of the next row.

Repeat the last row until all the stitches are worked off. Fasten off.

BACK

Make 7 ch.

1st row: As the 1st row of front. *2nd row:* Increase twice at the beginning and work to end.

Rep. the 2nd row until there are 49 loops on the hook at the end of the first part of the 22nd row. Break wool and leave loops on hook.

Make another piece of work in the same way. At the end of the first part of the 22nd row, work back as usual, make 2 ch., pick up the first piece of work, join the broken end of wool to the wool in use and then draw through all the loops.

23rd row: Increase once at each side of row.

Rep. the last row to end of 27th row.

28th row: Without increasing, work 3 rows.

Decrease once at each side of the next row.

Work 1 row. Rep. the last 2 rows up to the end of the 53rd row (88 sts.).

Work 2 rows. Decrease once at each side of the next row. Work the last 3 rows once more. Decrease once at each side of the next row. Work 1 row. Decrease once at each side of the next row. Work 3 rows. Decrease once at each side of the next row. Work 2 rows. Decrease once at each side of the next row. Work 4 rows. Decrease once at each side of the next row. Work 7 rows. Fasten off.

GUSSET

Make 3 ch.

1st row: As the 1st row of stitch instructions.

2nd row: Increase once at each side.

Rep. the 2nd row until there are 10 rows.

11th row: Without increasing.

12th row: Increase once at each side.

Rep. the last 2 rows until there are 15 rows.

Two rows without increasing.

18th row: Decrease once at each side.

Rep. the 18th row until there are three stitches left.

Fasten off. The first row of this gusset is stitched to the top of the opening at the commencement of the back.

BRASSIÈRE TOP

Make 26 ch. with red wool.

Turn and work 1 treble into the 4th ch. from hook and then rep. into every ch. to end.

2nd row: Turn each row with 3 ch. Work 1 treble into every treble of last row.

Rep. the 2nd row until there are 51 rows. Fasten off. Make another piece in this way.

TO MAKE UP

Sew up the side seams. Stitch in the gussets. Sew the two pieces of the brassière together. Stitch this to the top of the suit with the join in the centre back. There should be 11 rows of the treble loose at the front of the brassière. Catch the brassière together at the front point, turn each loose end down on to the right side of the work, making a point at each side. Fasten these points down with a button.

Now make 10 lengths of green ch. each 26 inches long. Thread each of these lengths of chain in and out of every treble row, each side of the brassière, leaving 4 treble between each threaded ch. Thread the ch. through alternate rows each time.

Make 2 or 3 yards of white ch. Thread this ch. in and out of every 4 treble rows across the rows of the brassière, threading over the 4 treble under which the ch. was threaded before. Work in this way until the ch. is finished and then continue to make lengths of ch. until all the brassière is threaded.

Wind the remaining green wool into 48 equal-sized balls. Take the thread from 24 of these balls and twist them into a tight cord. Take both ends of the cord in one hand and twist these two cords round each other very tightly. Measure off 36 inches of this cord and knot it at that point. Measure another 3 inches and cut it through here. Unravelling the ends to make a tassel, sew the end of the cord 3¾ inches from the centre back join of the brassière on the wrong side of the garment and then thread it through the turned-down piece of the brassière at the top front on the opposite side. Thread it through from the shoulder edge to the centre.

Make another cord in the same way and stitch it to the opposite side of the suit. And thread it through the other front.

With the terra-cotta wool, make a row of double crochet round the bottom of each leg.

A hank or two of wool, a little industry, and these joyous accessories are yours.

Wear A Waistcoat—

—crocheted by your own fair fingers, complete with matching cravat.

IF you would be smart (and who wouldn't ?) you simply *must* have a crocheted waistcoat and cravat to go with your Cardigan Suit.

I have drawn diagrams which speak more clearly than words —you will see that the cravat is joined to the back of the neck of the waistcoat.

Work your waistcoat and cravat in tricot stitch and use a light wool (light in weight) and, if possible, in a bright colour. This last only if your suit is light in colour.

Tricot Stitch.

WORK chain to length required. Turn.

Row 1 : 3 ch., 1 tr. into 1st stitch, 3 ch., 1 tr. into same stitch, * miss two stitches and work 1 tr., 3 ch., 1 tr. into next stitch.

Repeat from * all along the row.

Row 2: Work 1 tr., 3 ch., 1 tr., right through the space between each 2 trebles of previous row.

Repeat these two rows all along. For the waistcoat work vertically. For the scarf horizontally. Use a coarse bone hook so that the work is soft and pliable. It will take next to no time to do.

I HAVE seen vest and pantie sets crocheted in fine silk in semi-openwork stitch. They are terribly chic and so easy to do. You can work them out on any good paper pattern once you have gauged your stitch.

* * *

Crochet bust-bodices are the rage in Paris. Chanel is doing them in her very own shade of pink. Another idea you could work yourself.

* * *

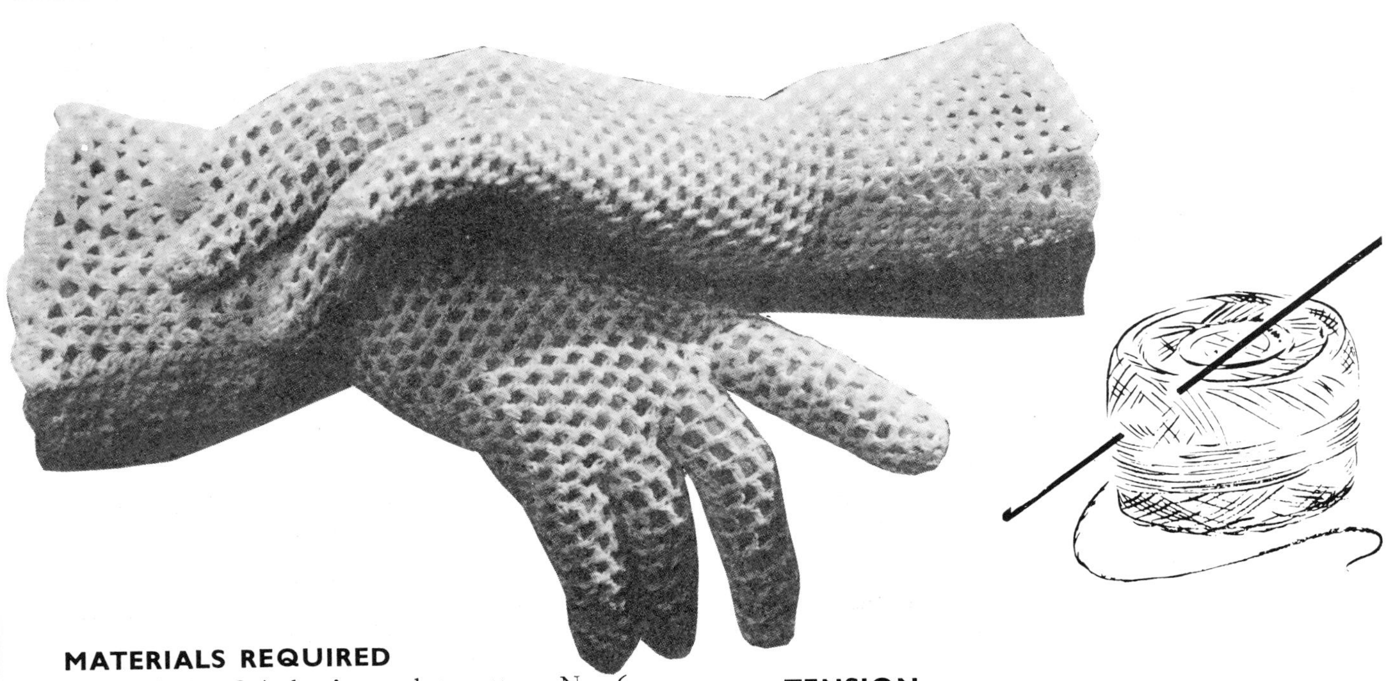

MATERIALS REQUIRED

Two balls of Ardern's crochet cotton, No. 6. A Milward's "Phantom" crochet hook, No. 14.

SIZES

Worked at the tension stated below, these gloves are equal to a $6\frac{1}{2}$–$6\frac{3}{4}$ size, but they may be made to fit any size by trying the unfinished glove on the hand from time to time and working more, or fewer, patterns and rows, in order to adjust the size of the glove to the size of the hand.

TENSION

Five patterns (of 1 ch., 1 tr.) make 1 inch in width, and four rows of this same pattern make 1 inch in depth, without stretching the work.

ABBREVIATIONS

Ch. chain; d.c. double crochet; tr. treble; s. slip; sp. space; inc. increase; dec. decrease; pat. pattern; tog. together.

Smart and dainty to wear with your summer frocks are the gloves crocheted in white crochet cotton; the pattern is very simple and they are terribly easy to make.

TO CROCHET

The Right Hand

The Thumb.—Make 4 ch., and s. into 1st ch. to form a ring.

1st round: 3 ch. (as 1 tr.), 10 tr. in the ring, s. into 3rd ch.

2nd round: (3 ch., 1 d.c. in next tr.) 11 times.

3rd round: S. into the middle of the next loop of 3 ch., 3 ch. (as 1 tr.), then (1 ch., 1 tr. in the next loop) to the end of the round, 1 ch., s. into 3rd ch. at beginning.

4th–8th rounds: S. into next sp. of previous round, 3 ch. (as 1 tr.), then (1 ch., 1 tr. in next sp.) to the end of the round, 1 ch., s. into 3rd ch. at beginning of round.

9th–12th rounds: As the 4th round, but inc. at the beginning of each round by working 2 pats. of (1 ch., 1 tr.) into the same sp. (15 sp.) Cut the cotton and leave the thumb.

The Fourth Finger.—Make 4 ch., and s. into 1st ch. to form a ring.

1st round: 3 ch., 8 tr. in the ring, s. into the 3rd ch.

2nd round: (3 ch., 1 d.c. in next tr.) 9 times.

3rd and 4th rounds: As 3rd and 4th rounds of thumb.

Repeat the 4th round for the length required. In the model there are 10 rounds altogether for the fourth finger. Cut the cotton.

The Third Finger.—Make 4 ch., s. into 1st ch. to form a ring.

1st round: 3 ch., 9 tr. in the ring. S. into the 3rd ch.

2nd round: (3 ch., 1 d.c. in next tr.) 10 times.

3rd round: As the 3rd round of the thumb.

4th–12th rounds (or the required length)*:* As the 4th round of the thumb.

Place this finger beside the previous finger, and join them by working a d.c. into 1 sp. from both fingers, at the base, taken tog., then (1 ch., 1 d.c. into the next sp. of both fingers taken tog.) twice. Fasten off.

The Second Finger.—This is the same as the third finger, but with 1 more round. Join it to the base of the third finger, along 3 sp., so that there are 2 unjoined sp. along the front, and 2 unjoined sp. along the back of the hand, at the base of the third finger. Fasten off.

The First Finger.—As the second finger, and join it to the base of the second finger, but do not cut the cotton.

The Hand.—*1st round:* 3 ch. (as 1 tr.), then (1 ch., 1 tr.) into each of the next 7 sp. at the base of the first finger. Now work a Y-shaped stitch into the 2 sp. which were joined at the base of the first and second fingers, thus, * 1 ch., cotton over hook, insert hook into joined sp. of first finger and draw cotton through the sp., cotton over hook, draw it through 2 loops on hook, cotton over hook, insert hook in joined sp. of second finger and draw cotton through the sp., (cotton over hook and draw it through 2 loops on hook) 3 times.* (1 ch., 1 tr. in next sp. of second finger) twice, work from * to * into the 2 joined sp. of the second and third fingers, (1 ch., 1 tr. in next sp. of third finger) twice, work from * to * in the 2 joined sp. of the third and fourth fingers, (1 ch., 1 tr. in next sp. of fourth finger) 6 times, work from * to * into the joined sp. of the fourth and third fingers, (1 ch., 1 tr. into next sp. of third finger) twice, work from * to * into joined sp. of third and second fingers, (1 ch., 1 tr. in next sp. of second finger) twice, 1 ch., s. into 3rd ch. at beginning of round. (27 sp.)

Next 3 rounds: As 4th round of thumb.

Next round: In the (1 ch., 1 tr.) pat., and inc. 1 sp. just below the first finger, by working (1 ch., 1 tr.) twice into 1 sp.

Next 2 rounds: In pat.

Next round: Inc. 1 sp. just below the first finger.

Next round: In pat.

To Join the Thumb.—Place the glove on the right hand, and mark the 4 sp. along which the thumb should be joined.

1st round: Work in pat. as before, but while proceeding along the 4 marked sp., place the beginning of the last round of the thumb along these 4 sp., and join the thumb and hand in the same way as the fingers. Finish the round.

2nd round: Work in pat. along the hand, until the join is reached, work from * to * as in the 1st round of the hand, (1 ch., 1 tr. in next sp. of base of thumb) 11 times. Work from * to *, and finish the round along the hand. (37 sp.)

3rd round: Work in pat. until the sp. immediately before the Y-shaped stitch of previous round is reached, then dec. by working from * to *, thus working 1 pat. into the next 2 sp., in the same way as 1 pat. was worked into 2 joined sp., 10 sp., dec., finish the round. (35 sp.)

4th and 5th rounds: In pat.

6th round: As the 3rd round, with 9 sp. between the decs. *7th and 8th rounds:* In pat.

9th round: As the 3rd round, with 8 sp. between the decs.

10th and 11th rounds: In pat., and omit the 1 ch. at the end of the 11th round, and s. into the 3rd ch. at beginning, to make 30 sp.

The Gauntlet.—*1st round:* S. into next sp., 3 ch. (as 1 tr.), 1 tr. in same sp., 2 ch., 2 tr. in next sp., (2 tr. in next sp., 2 ch., 2 tr. in next sp.) 14 times, s. into 3rd ch.

2nd round: 3 ch., (2 tr. in next sp., 2 ch., 2 tr. in the same sp., 1 tr. in the hole between the next 2 sets of 2 tr. which have no ch. between them) 14 times, (2 tr., 2 ch., 2 tr.) in the next sp., s. into the 3rd ch.

3rd–7th rounds: 3 ch., (2 tr., 2 ch., 2 tr., all into the next sp., 1 tr. in the single tr. between 2 sets of 2 tr.) 14 times, (2 tr., 2 ch., 2 tr.) in next sp., s. into 3rd ch.

8th–10th rounds: As the 3rd round, but with 3 ch. instead of 2 ch. between the 2 sets of 2 tr.

11th round: 3 ch., (1 tr. in each of next 2 tr., 3 tr. in sp., 1 tr. in each of next 3 tr.) until the round is completed. S. into 3rd ch. and fasten off.

The Left Hand.—This is the same as the right hand, but when joining the thumb, try the glove on the left hand to mark the 4 sp. along which the thumb is to be joined.

Press the gloves into shape under a damp cloth.

IT'S VERY SIMPLE TO MAKE

AN UP-TO-THE-MINUTE
MODEL IN CRYSTAL RAFFIA

Materials.—1 oz. (two ½-oz. cards) of "Crystal" Raffia Art. E.960, and a steel crochet hook No. 1.
Measurements.—Width round head, 22 inches.
Tension.—7 d.c. to 1 inch in width and 10 rounds to 1 inch in depth.
Abbreviations.—Ch. = chain; d.c. = double crochet; tr. = treble; rep. = repeat; st. = stitch.

BEGIN in the centre of the crown. Make 4 ch., then work 6 d.c. into the 4th ch. from the hook. Join into a ring with a slip-stitch and also join every following round in the same way.

1st round.—2 d.c. into each d.c.

2nd round.—* 1 d.c. into the first d.c., 2 d.c. into the next. Rep. from * all round.

3rd round.—* 1 d.c. into the first 2 d.c., 2 d.c. into the next. Rep. from * all round.

4th round.—* 1 d.c. into the first 3 d.c., 2 d.c. into the next. Rep. from * all round.

Continue to increase in this way until you have worked the 8th round and have 54 d.c. in all.

9th round.—3 ch. to stand for the 1st tr., then work 2 tr. into same st.; * 1 ch., miss 2 d.c., 3 tr. into the next d.c. Rep. from * all round.

10th round.—* 1 ch., 1 d.c. into the middle of the 3 tr., 1 ch., 3 tr. into the space between the tr. below. Rep. from * all round.

11th round.—Same as 10th, but work the 3 tr. into the first space between the 3 tr. and 1 d.c. Now work 11 rounds of d.c., increasing at intervals always in the same place in every round, to keep the beret flat.

23rd round.—3 tr. into a st., * 1 ch., miss 2 d.c., 3 tr. into the next d.c. Rep. from * all round.

24th round.—Like the 10th round, but miss 1 ch. between tr. and d.c.

Now work 11 rounds of d.c., st. into st.

27th round.—Like 23rd round.

28th round.—* 3 tr. in the space, 1 ch. Rep. all round.

29th round.—Like 28th round.

Now work 12 rounds of d.c., taking 2 d.c. together at intervals in each round to decrease, then work 6 rounds st. into st. Cut the raffia and darn in the end. If a larger or smaller head circle is required dec. accordingly.

For the bow. Make 2 ch., then work 2 d.c. into each ch.

2nd row.—2 d.c. into the first d.c., 1 d.c. into the next 2 d.c., 2 d.c. into the last d.c.

3rd row.—2 d.c. into the first d.c., 4 d.c., 2 d.c. into the last 2 d.c.

Now work row upon row of 8 d.c. until you have a sufficient length to make a bow, decreasing at this end to match the other.

Press the beret on the wrong side with a warm iron, then fold the bow and sew to the left side. Turn up the last 6 rounds inside and press back to make a firm edge.

CHAIN.

DOUBLE-CROCHET.

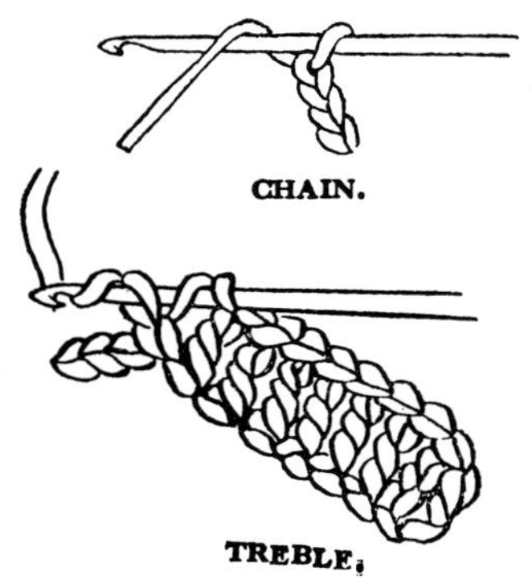

TREBLE.

HERE YOU SEE EXACTLY HOW TO WORK THE STITCHES.